Catholic Women Preach

Catholic Women Preach

Raising Voices, Renewing the Church

CYCLE A

Elizabeth Donnelly and Russ Petrus, Editors

ORBIS BOOKS
Maryknoll, New York 10545

Library of Congress Cataloging-in-Publication Data

Names: Donnelly, Elizabeth A., editor. | Russ, Petrus, editor.
Title: Catholic women preach : raising voices, renewing the church--Cycle A / Elizabeth A. Donnelly and Petrus Russ.
Description: Maryknoll, NY : Orbis Books, 2022. | Series: Catholic women preach ; Cycle A | Includes bibliographical references. | Summary: "Homilies by Catholic women following the Sunday lectionary readings for Cycle A"-- Provided by publisher.
Identifiers: LCCN 2022014472 (print) | LCCN 2022014473 (ebook) | ISBN 9781626984837 | ISBN 9781608339457 (epub)
Subjects: LCSH: Catholic Church--Sermons. | Church year sermons. | Common lectionary (1992). Year A. | Sermons--Women authors.
Classification: LCC BX1756.A2 C38 2022 (print) | LCC BX1756.A2 (ebook) | DDC 252/.02--dc23/eng/20220613
LC record available at https://lccn.loc.gov/2022014472
LC ebook record available at https://lccn.loc.gov/2022014473

Contents

CHRISTMAS SEASON

LENT

EASTER SEASON

ORDINARY TIME

Editors' note: Homilies in this volume were given during Cycle A in previous years, when in some cases (here the ninth through eleventh Sundays in Ordinary Time) solemnities took precedence over Sundays.

CONTENTS

CONTENTS

Foreword

Barbara E. Reid, OP

Among all the various ministries, there is none more crucial than the ministry of the Word. Jesus began his mission by preaching the good news (Mark 1:14–15; Luke 4:16–18), and he sent the first apostles to do the same (Luke 9:2). At Pentecost, the first thing that happens to the Spirit-filled followers of Jesus is that they begin to speak in all different languages about God's deeds of power (Acts 2:1–11). And when Paul lists the various ministries, first and foremost are apostles, prophets, and teachers (1 Cor 12:28).

The New Testament and other early Christian traditions give us abundant evidence of women who were preachers, teachers, prophets, and evangelizers in the early days of the Jesus movement. Luke's Gospel opens with prophetic women preaching powerfully liberating words. Mary, the mother of Jesus, praises God for past saving deeds and proclaims the way toward peace and well-being for all (Luke 1:46–55). Her Magnificat is still recited and sung daily by Christians worldwide. Elizabeth proclaims that there is blessedness in the most difficult of circumstances (Luke 1:39–45) and that God's delight is in taking away affliction (1:25). And at the circumcision and naming of her son, her proclamation of God's grace (the literal meaning of her son's name is "grace of God") has the effect of bringing her husband to fuller faith, enabling him to speak again and to praise God. Not only that, but Elizabeth's words cause all those present and people all throughout the hill country of Judea to marvel at God's mighty deeds (Luke 1:59–66). The prophet Anna, who kept vigil in the temple for eighty-four years, continuously preached hope to all who were looking for redemption (Luke 2:36–38).

Mary Magdalene and the other Galilean women who followed Jesus and ministered with him were the first to be commissioned by him to preach the good news (Matt 28:1–10; John 20:1–2, 11–18). The Samaritan woman preached to her townspeople, who came to believe in Jesus because of her word (John 4:39). In Orthodox tradition, she is named Photina, "Enlightened One," and is said to be "equal to the apostles." Junia, a relative of Paul, was "prominent among the apostles," presumably preaching far and wide, as did Paul, and for which she pays the price of imprisonment with him (Rom 16:7). Phoebe, *diakonos* of the church of Cenchreae, would undoubtedly have overseen and shared in the preaching to and evangelizing of this harbor community at the port of Corinth (Rom 16:1–3). Prisca, along with her husband Aquila, must have herself been a prominent preacher and teacher, as she explained more accurately the way of God to Apollos, an eloquent preacher from Alexandria (Acts 18:26). Euodia and Syntyche worked mightily alongside Paul in evangelizing at Philippi (Phil 4:2–3). While neither their names nor the content of their proclamations are preserved, Philip's four daughters were prophets (Acts 21:9), as were a number of Corinthian women (1 Cor 11:5).

Extracanonical traditions preserve the memory of women itinerant preachers such as Thecla and Nino. The *Acts of Thecla*, for example, written in Asia Minor in the late second century, tells of how Thecla, a rich aristocratic woman from Iconium, renounced her family, fortune, and fiancé to join Paul in his apostolic mission, preaching to both men and women. Devotion to her became widespread throughout Asia Minor and Egypt, particularly among women, who saw her as a model of empowerment. Another woman venerated in the Orthodox Church as "equal of the apostles" is Nino or Nina. Juvenal, the first patriarch of Jerusalem (451–458), gave her a cross and commissioned her to evangelize wherever she might go. She made her way to Georgia (ancient Iberia), making converts of all who heard her preaching, including Queen Nana, and eventually King Mirian, who declared Christianity the official religion.

Just as these early women followers of Jesus took to heart his commission to preach the good news, so women have continued to do throughout Christian history. Women disciples know that our charism to preach is grounded in our baptism and confirmation. Gifted further with theological education, pastoral experience, and a listening heart, we can do no less than share this gift as widely as we can. While inadequate interpretations of scripture and patriarchal understandings of the order of creation and of ecclesial structures currently continue to restrict women's ability to exercise the preaching ministry, the Spirit always finds a way for the word to be preached.

The preachers included in this volume represent a vast array of communities of believers of diverse races, geographic areas, economic strata, sexual orientations, and cultures. And whether physical or spiritual mothers, each does as Pope Francis urges in *Evangelii Gaudium*, "the Church . . . preaches in the same way that a mother speaks to her child. . . . Just as all of us like to be spoken to in our mother tongue, so too, in the faith we like to be spoken to in our 'mother culture' . . . and our heart is better disposed to listen" (#139). As you listen with the ear of your heart to the wisdom of women, may you, too, be emboldened to preach the word with persistence at all times and in all ways.

Introduction

Elizabeth Donnelly and Russ Petrus

The Holy Spirit is at work in wondrous ways. And sometimes we are blessed to be awake and receptive to the Spirit's direction. Such is the story of *Catholic Women Preach*, which came to life when the Spirit led faith-filled travelers on similar journeys.

One night in 2013, Betty Anne Donnelly found herself unable to sleep, energized by her reflection upon an experience she had in 2011 while serving on the Women's Advisory Committee of the Woodstock Theological Center in Washington, DC. The distinguished fellows—lay women and men, vowed religious and priests—were committed to communal theological reflection on pressing issues. They felt strongly that women's voices were not being heard in the Catholic Church, a fact that served to impoverish the whole church. They determined to film Betty Anne and three other women on the advisory committee preaching on the readings for the four Sundays of Advent that year.

It was daunting and thrilling to be filmed by the talented documentarians Mary and Frank Frost in the gorgeous Copley Crypt Chapel on Georgetown University's campus. Each woman wore a purple—or in Kerry Robinson's case, pink—stole to mark the solemnity and joy of the liturgical season. The Woodstock team posted the preaching videos on their website, publicized them in their newsletter, and received ample positive feedback from their supporters.

Lying awake one night, Betty Anne was inspired by a bold idea: to scale up this series and develop a website featuring gifted Catholic women from around the world, diverse in age and ethnicity, preaching on the readings for each Sunday and certain feast days throughout the year.

Meanwhile, FutureChurch board members Jocelyn Collen, Diana Culbertson, OP, and Rita Houlihan had set out with executive director Deborah Rose to expand upon the organization's "Unheard Homilies" project. Introduced as a part of FutureChurch's Annual Mary of Magdala Celebrations in 2001, "Unheard Homilies" created a space for women preachers to publicly reflect on the Word of God at a time when lay preaching (while permitted under canon law) was being stifled in many parts of the Church. FutureChurch began posting these "unheard homilies" from Mary of Magdala Celebrations on its website. Encouraged by abundant positive feedback, the board of FutureChurch decided to expand the work by creating an online platform for Catholic women to preach.

In 2015, Deborah Rose and Betty Anne met and shared their common pursuit of raising the voices of Catholic women through preaching. Russ Petrus, then program director for FutureChurch, brought his web development skills into the mix and designed what would become the platform for Catholic Women Preach. After a year of planning and development, the Catholic Women Preach website (https://www.catholicwomenpreach.org/) officially launched in November of 2016 with preaching for Advent.

Since the launching of the website, well over three hundred extraordinary Catholic women have blessed us with challenging and inspiring reflections. All of their contributions remain fully accessible on the website, representing a rich trove of wisdom to browse and search.

This project could not have been successful without the help of our distinguished advisory board members: M. Shawn

Copeland; Richard Gaillardetz; Thomas Groome; Nontando Hadebe; Mary Catherine Hilkert, OP; James Keenan, SJ; Raymond Kemp; Paul Lakeland; Astrid Lobo Gajiwala; James Martin, SJ; Rhonda Miska; Carolyn Osiek, RSCJ; Brian Pierce, OP; Nancy Pineda-Madrid; Barbara Reid, OP; Kerry Robinson; Christine Schenk, CSJ; and June Siciliano, OP.

We are also grateful for those who offered editorial assistance: Diana Culbertson, OP; Marianne Race, CSJ; Janet Schlichting, OP; and Mary Ann Wiesemann-Mills, OP.

We are extremely grateful to Robert Ellsberg for encouraging us to edit this collection of Year A homilies. We could not have done it without the assistance of the extraordinarily talented and tenacious Kelly Sankowski, who corresponded with our contributors, proposed homily titles, and edited and updated biographies. Our warmest thanks to Kelly.

We dedicate this volume to the many prophetic, Spirit-led women who have inspired and helped to clear and illuminate a path forward for us. Three contributors to this volume—Louise Akers, SC; Francine Cardman, PhD; and Jeannie Masterson, CSJ—completed their earthly journeys before they could see their work published. May they be among the cloud of witnesses who continue to guide us and help us discern the stirrings of the Spirit.

ADVENT

First Sunday of Advent

Stay awake!

Jamie T. Phelps, OP

Isaiah 2:1–5
Psalm 122: 1–2, 3–4, 4–5, 6–7, 8–9
Romans 13:11–14
Matthew 24:37–44

The readings for the first Sunday of Advent admonish us to stay awake. They call us to be attentive to what is happening in our place and in our times. Today, I am very conscious of the human divisions within our global world and nation.

Recent events across our world and nation reveal serious divisions within the family of God. Wars in the Middle East and the ongoing Palestinian-Israeli conflict manifest religious divisions among Christians, Muslims, and Jews. Large scale immigration reveals religious oppression as families leave their homelands to seek peace and the recognition of their equality and dignity as human beings. Diversity of race, nationality, and culture become terms of division rather than enrichment. Most prominent in our news media are the race and class divisions. The rich, predominantly white, minority has access to quality housing, education, and ownership of goods as well as control of our corporations and social institutions. The poor, on the other hand, lack quality housing, education, possessions, and decision making or participation in our major corporations and social institutions.

The wealthy are more visible and exercise power and control over our nation. The middle class is diminishing. The number of the poor is increasing. The wisdom, gifts, talents, and power of the poor are denied and/or rendered invisible and ineffective as the poor are relegated to the margins. The availability of quality housing, food, and education varies in accord with one's class, race, national identity, and location in the world. Unemployment, homelessness, and poverty are increasing.

Gang violence among and between Black, Latino, Asian, and Euro-American gangs and police brutality reveal ethnic-racial and class division and systemic oppression. Secularity, the denial of the existence of God's presence and role in our lives, is increasing and is accompanied by a rise in personal narcissism, materialism, and social indifference to the common good. Racism, sexism, nationalism, imperialism, and capitalism divide the human community. Some individuals and groups, such as the Ku Klux Klan, claim superiority or dominance over others based on their skin color, gender, economic status, or nation of origin.

The reality of anti-Black bigotry and hatred of African Americans, Hispanic Americans, and Native Americans was made plain in our recent election as both candidates accused one another and both parties of racial and class bias and bigotry. *Division, bigotry, and hatred contradict the will and way of God!*

In the readings for the first Sunday of Advent, God calls us to walk in the light. God calls us to stay awake to God's presence in our life and in the lives of others. God calls us to stay awake to the presence of the divine manifested in our daily lives.

God calls us to embody God's universal, unconditional love. Only then does our true identity as the People of God become visible. We are made in the image and likeness of the Triune God: three distinct persons bound by the common identity of God. We are called to reflect in our lives the same unity/diversity that characterizes God.

As we begin this Advent season in preparation for the rebirth and/or deepening of our consciousness of Jesus in our lives and in our world:

Let us expand our circle of those included in our love of God and love of neighbor.

Let us "wake up and stay awake" by being attentive and seeking to construct and strengthen our individual, national, and global relationships.

Let us seek to mend our divisions by seeking to engage those who are different from ourselves and thus prepare for that unity in community that characterizes the coming of God's kingdom in our midst every day.

Let us heed Psalm 122 and "Put on the Lord Jesus Christ..."

Let us "Pray for the peace!"

Let us "throw off the works of darkness and put on the armor of light; let us conduct ourselves properly as in the day, not in orgies and drunkenness, not in promiscuity and lust, not in rivalry and jealousy."

Let us live in accord with the words of chapter 24 of Matthew's Gospel which admonishes us to "stay awake! For you do not know on which day your Lord will come. Be sure of this: if the master of the house had known the hour of night when the thief was coming, he would have stayed awake and not let his house be broken into. So too, you also must be prepared, for at an hour you do not expect, the Son of Man will come."

If we stay awake, we will remain attentive to and embody God's will and way, and our song will be the song of the psalmist. We too will sing with joy as we go to the house of the Lord!

R. Let us go rejoicing to the house of the Lord!

Second Sunday of Advent
A change of direction

Astrid Lobo Gajiwala

Isaiah 11:1–10
Psalm 72:1–2, 7–8, 12–13, 17
Romans 15:4–9
Matthew 3:1–12

At the time of working on this reflection, India was celebrating its only medals at the Rio Olympics, a bronze and a silver won by the twenty-three-year-old wrestler Sakshi Malik and the twenty-one-year-old shuttler, P.V. Sindhu. A third contestant, the twenty-three-year-old gymnast Dipa Karmarkar, who missed a medal by a whisker, held her country spellbound as she did the "vault of death" that is rarely attempted. One headline I particularly liked was, "They fought like girls."

To understand their real triumph you have to view it against the background of their lives—being born girls in "gender critical" states where baby girls are literally killed before they can dream (forget about allowing them to follow their dreams). They took up their sport against the patriarchal and medieval protests of the entire village that considered such sport "not meant for girls." They faced flak for the figure-hugging, skin-revealing outfits that were a must for their sport. And single girls traveling outside the village, especially in the company of men, was just not done. These women surmounted the odds of no funding; homemade, makeshift equipment; and no guidance. They made it through sheer grit, passion, and faith. They brought pride to a nation that had almost given up hope of victory.

We are called to participate in God's redemptive plan
In the gospel of the second Sunday of Advent we meet a character cast in the same mold as these plucky Indian women—John the Baptist. Like them, he is single-minded in his purpose. His mission is his life, and he is willing to give his life for it. A maverick, he too refuses to conform. He emerges from the wilderness clothed in camel's hair and a leather belt around his waist. His food is simple, neither bread nor wine (Matt 11:18; Luke 7:33), only locusts and wild honey (Matt 3:4; Mark 1:6). His very lifestyle in its austerity proclaims the counter-culture he has come to announce, one that places little value on the preoccupations of the world.

While still in his mother's womb, John was chosen to be God's ambassador and he carries this consciousness of being set apart into adulthood, strengthening it with self-discipline and penance. Like those Olympic champions, he prepares vigorously for that great moment when he will make an appearance on life's stage, when all will be watching. For four hundred years there had been no prophet in the Jewish world, and now he is here proclaiming the advent of one who will bring justice for the poor, liberation for the afflicted, and vengeance to the oppressor (Isa 11:3–5). He is the forerunner of the Christ, who, as Saint Paul tells us in the second reading, brings hope and salvation to all—Jews and Gentiles alike.

We are called to be open to God's grace and action
John's desert experience is central to his mission. If he is to be a participant in God's redemptive plan, he must open himself

up to God's grace and action. In the stillness of his heart, he must hear God's voice. And so he goes into the wilderness, away from all distraction, to meet his God. How many of us do this—go into the wilderness, find spaces of silence in our day, away from thoughts, desires, ambitions, plans? Do we think about emptying ourselves so that we may be filled with the Spirit? Do we make time to look within and feel the pull of the heart? Sadly, such quietness is not a priority for most of us. It is not even on our "to-do" list. We are so busy with family, home, work, or connecting with friends on social media. "Work is prayer," we console ourselves. Even our parishes are frequently caught up in this whirlwind of activity. Pope John Paul II repeatedly stressed that Catholic parishes are meant to be "genuine schools of prayer," where the "art" of prayer is taught and learned. But how many of our parishes see this as a key point in pastoral planning?

The gospels tell us that Jesus often took off on his own to pray, away from his disciples, away from the multitudes that constantly followed him. He went up into the mountains to pray (Matt 14:22–23; Mark 6:45–46; John 6:15), sometimes staying there all night (Luke 6:12–13); he woke up before the break of dawn to pray (Mark 1:35); he retreated into the wilderness to pray (Luke 4:42; 5:16). Watching him pray, his disciples were moved to ask, "Lord, teach us to pray as John also taught his disciples" (Luke 11:1). Reflecting on this we are probably tempted to say, "Jesus was God and John was special, so it was easy for them. But life is so different today."

So let's take a woman of our times, Mother Teresa of Kolkata, who was recently canonized. When asked about the success of her work she confessed, "I don't think that I could do this work for even one week if I didn't have four hours of prayer every day." And what was this prayer like? When an interviewer asked her, "When you pray, what do you say to

God?" she answered simply, "I don't talk, I simply listen." When he persisted, "Ah, then what is it that God says to you when you pray?" she replied, "God also doesn't talk. God also simply listens." Four hours every day. Besides tending to the dying and unwanted, she was directing her congregation and establishing foundations across the world. By the time she died in 1997, she had 610 foundations in 123 countries. She obviously was a very busy woman. Yet, she made the time to enter into the calmness of the Spirit.

This plugging into the Spirit is part of John's life too. In the solitude of the desert, the Spirit of the Lord rests upon him enabling him to set forth as the one who goes before, to prepare for the one who is to come. People come from "Jerusalem, all Judea, and the whole region around the Jordan" to listen to him and be baptized by him. They are moved to acknowledge their sins. All because they experience the power of God in him. His is the voice crying in the wilderness, as foretold by the prophet Isaiah: "Make ready the way of the Lord, make his paths straight (so that) all flesh will see the salvation of God" (Luke 3:4–6). What does it mean to make his paths straight?

We are called to destroy the enemy within

When John is baptizing his people, Jesus is already there in their midst. But the Jewish religious leaders do not see him. They do not recognize him because he does not fit their idea of a messiah. Initially they longed for a deliverer, one who would free them from their oppressors. But as time went by they also wanted an avenger, one who would destroy their enemies.

However, the messiah who comes is looking to liberate the Jews from another kind of enemy, one that is within. He has come to destroy hypocrisy, greed, selfishness, and obsession with cultic purity and lineage, and his forerunner, John the Baptist, prepares the way by pointing out the ravines into which the people have fallen, and the hills and mountains that block the path to salvation. He prepares the way by drawing attention to the obstacles to God's arrival.

We are called to change direction

John comes preaching a baptism of repentance for the forgiveness of sins. He gets people to start reflecting on their lives and their relationship with God. The first-century historian Josephus writes, "John enjoined upon the Jews *first* to cultivate virtue and to put into practice righteousness toward one another and piety toward God, and *then* to come to his baptism, for thus only would the baptism be acceptable to God." So the repentance John asks for is more than just remorse and regret. The repentance he asks for is *metanoia*, the Greek term for "a change of mind." It involves first of all recognition of our wicked ways and unrighteous thoughts (Isa 55:7), whether through commission or omission (Jas 4:17; Luke 10:30–37; Matt 25:31–46). This admission of wrongdoing must be accompanied by an acknowledgment of personal responsibility and a desire for cleansing the heart and restoring right relationship with God. It is only when all these elements are present in the inward response that an outward change of behavior is possible. Only then can we change direction by "turning away" from what is wrong and "turning to" God.

We are called to set the world in the right direction

Interestingly, the Pharisees and Sadducees too flocked to John's baptism in large numbers. They were the religious elite of Jerusalem. They followed all the rules, never skipped worship, performed the rituals meticulously and came from families that went all the way back to Abraham. Their presence should have made John happy; by coming to him they were, in a way, giving him credibility. Instead, John saw right through them and called them a "brood of vipers."

He was not deceived by their outward religiosity. He knew that they were not there to repent, but to take an easy way out. They were there because their rabbis had foretold that the Messiah's advent would be preceded by a period of great suffering, generally known as the "woes of Messiah," and they thought John's baptism was an easy ritual that would protect them from the "woes." But John immediately called them out: "Produce good fruit as evidence of your repentance," he challenged them (Matt 3:8). And lest they think that having Abraham as their father was enough to presume relationship with God, he quickly disillusioned them. "God can raise up children to Abraham from these stones," he told them.

It is a reminder for us too who are complacent in our baptism, believing that it is our passport to heaven. No amount of pious devotions and reception of the sacraments can substitute for the true *metanoia* that will bring about God's reign of righteousness and right relationship. Like John and Jesus, we too must be symbols of God's initiative taking shape in the world. Like them, we must challenge unjust structures and practices that promote discrimination on the basis of race, class, caste, religion, and gender. We must begin to question the world economy that Pope Francis points out perpetuates a fundamental terrorism against all humanity by placing at its center the god of money. We must feel moved to open the doors of mercy to those who come to us in need—the poor, the unwanted, the broken, the migrant, the refugee. And we must be ever conscious of the need to heal and safeguard Mother Earth against greed and selfish exploitation. As we change direction in our lives, its impact must be evident in the way we view the world and respond to its concerns. We must strive too to set the world in the right direction.

We are called to point a way to God
The season of Advent provides us with an opportunity for new beginnings. It blends a penitential theme with one of prayer-

ful, spiritual preparation for the second and final coming of our Lord, and one of joyful anticipation of the celebration of the Incarnation and Christ's birth. It is a time for looking within and asking: What must we change to make a way for the Lord in our hearts and in our world? But it is also a season of looking forward, of moving toward something greater. In the gospel reading, John directs us to Jesus as the one who is mightier than he, the one who will baptize with the Holy Spirit and fire and bring new life not just to the Jews but to all who call on His name. Today's gospel invites us to stand like John, passionate and steadfast in the face of criticism, temptation, ridicule, and even persecution, and point a way to Jesus Christ through the choices we make, the values we live by, the causes we uphold.

The fruit of such repentance and right living is reconciliation. In the first reading the prophet Isaiah tells us about a new world order that will be ushered in by the Messiah, one that will be characterized by justice, faithfulness, and kinship across all boundaries. In this reconciled world there will be no enmity—predators will live in peace with their prey and their young will browse together; there will be no discrimination—the strong and the weak will share the same meal; and there will be no fear—the vulnerable will be protected, for "the earth shall be filled with knowledge of the Lord, as water covers the sea" (Isa 11:9). This is the promise of Advent.

Third Sunday of Advent

Celebrating what is good

KERRY A. ROBINSON

Isaiah 35:1–6A, 10
Psalm 146:6–7, 8–9, 9–10
James 5:7–10
Matthew 11:2–11

Today is Gaudete Sunday—the Sunday of joy, as Pope Francis refers to it. Gaudete—in Latin—means rejoice. All over the world on this day, Christian churches are celebrating Gaudete Sunday.

Admittedly, we are halfway through the Advent Season and many of us are laboring under the preparations and the added responsibilities that come with anticipating Christmas. Admittedly, too, when we think of a day of rejoicing, perhaps our hearts aren't fully in it at this particular moment.

Gaudete is symbolized by the color rose. We see that reflected in the vestments of the celebrant and in the color of the candle in our Advent wreath that we light today. Pink. Joy. Rejoicing. What do we make of the injunction to be joyful right now as constitutive of being a person of faith, especially when our hearts might not be in it? Henri Nouwen makes the distinction between happiness, which is contingent on external circumstances, and joy, which is entirely conditioned by the interior disposition. Henri argues that this kind of funda-mental interior joy, not dependent on external circumstances, is possible only in response to one fundamental faith question. Do you believe—radically believe—in a loving God who loves you just for who you are, unconditionally and unfailingly? A positive answer to that question will set the conditions for an interior life of joy, even, and especially, in the midst of pro-found suffering.

I know that many of us might be arriving at this point in Advent, today, with very heavy hearts. I know that some of us have lost people very close to us and anticipate the holi-days for the first time without our beloved friend, or daugh-ter, or mother. I also know that there is anxiety around meaningful work, the ability to provide for our families, the end of important relationships. There are endless reasons that one might be arriving at this day unsettled, unnerved, anx-ious, and deeply sorrowful. Communally, when we step back and we look at our neighborhoods, at our cities, at our coun-tries, and at our world, what do we see? What is the cause of so much suffering and anxiety? We bear witness to daily ex-amples of sexism, of racism, of woeful ignorance of the plight of refugees and migrants, of the homeless in our very midst. These are all reasons that would dampen the human heart and cause great anguish.

And yet, today we are called to be joyful. How? How can that be possible?

Let's look at the gospel reading in this context. It is dra-matic. It opens with John the Baptist, the greatest of the New Testament prophets. He has been tremendously faithful in his mission. He is Jesus's cousin. He is the messenger of Christ. And here he is, in jail. It doesn't look, from his perspective, like things turned out the way he thought they might. So he sends his disciples to Jesus asking one question: "Jesus, are you the one we have been waiting for? Or should we look for another?" It is a profound admission of doubt on the part of John the Baptist. I think this gives us permission today to see doubt in our faith lives as profoundly holy and deeply meaningful. If we want to have an adult mature life of faith, doubt is good. It is important. It is part of wrestling with the big questions of meaning and our purpose in the universe.

Jesus's response is even more interesting. He doesn't send John's disciples back with evidence of how he has conquered and vanquished with his almighty power. Instead he points to the fruit of his labor, the fruit of God's agency working through him. And what is that fruit? It's all about healing and reconciliation and extending mercy to those on the margins and bringing good news to the poor. Shocking, but constitutive of what it means to be Christian. And that is the invitation to belong to this great community of faith that Jesus has initiated.

I have a wonderful friend, Mary Ann Wasil, who was diagnosed with breast cancer twelve years ago. This was her favorite day, Gaudete Sunday, not only because the color associated with it is pink, which is also the color associated with the many efforts to promote breast health advocacy across the globe, but because of her fundamental belief in a beautiful, benevolent, loving God who was always at her side. She took the worst thing that she could have imagined and suffered—the diagnosis of breast cancer—and rather than let herself sink into the mire of this sorrow, she converted it to be a blessing for others. She, out of her faithful relationship with Christ, decided to take this and offer it as a blessing to girls and women all over the world. That was an example that gave rise to hope and encouragement and love and consolation for so many. And this is what we are being asked to do on this day. No matter what sorrows are in our heart. No matter what we have brought here on this Gaudete Sunday. We each face the fundamental question before us: Do you believe in a God who so lavishly loves you just for being you, whose love for you is unfailing? And if your answer is yes, can you let yourself be a blessing to others, be a hope for others?

Ultimately, this day of rejoicing is about celebrating what is good in order to find the strength to fix what is wrong.

Happy Gaudete Sunday.

Fourth Sunday of Advent

Taking the long route

NONTANDO HADEBE

Isaiah 7:10–14
Psalm 24:1–12, 3–14, 5–16
Romans 1:1–17
Matthew 1:18–124

> "If you want to go fast, go alone. If you want to go
> far, go together." —African proverb

I have used an African proverb to bring together my reflections on the readings of this Fourth Sunday of Advent. In oral cultures, proverbs are the prime ethical teaching tools because they are easy to remember and contain multiple meanings, thus making them rich sources for reflection. This particular proverb is no different. It can be interpreted in many ways, but for the purposes of this reflection I will be focusing on the importance of partnership, or working with others, instead of working alone in order to build and sustain long-term goals. Working alone is easier and tasks are done much faster because one does not need to engage, negotiate, and seek consensus or cooperation with others. Yet this proverb makes the claim that work for a goal that is long-term and sustainable requires the participation of others in a shared vision.

So does this rule apply to God? Does God operate alone, without engaging humanity in the work of salvation?

In the reading from Isaiah, God is in conversation with King Ahaz and makes a promise for the future coming of Emmanuel—God with us. In the gospel reading, the coming and mission of Emmanuel are revealed in conversation with Joseph and prior to that in conversation with Mary. Jesus is Emmanuel. It would have been easier for God to make Jesus appear as an adult and carry out his ministry. But God chooses to "go far"—to take the long route of working with others, being vulnerable, entering into conversation, involving strangers in God's plan. The coming of Emmanuel caused a rift in the relationship between Mary and Joseph. God stepped in through a dream to enter a conversation with Joseph that explained the pregnancy of Mary and the destiny of Emmanuel as Jesus, the one who would save humanity from their sins. Emmanuel came as a baby, not an adult, and had to grow in a family, which required the support and love of Mary and Joseph, family, and community.

Yeshua had to grow until he was an adult before he could proclaim the gospel of salvation. All this took time. A promise made centuries ago was fulfilled through participation of others and their sacrifice and willingness to be part of the plan of salvation.

In the Letter to the Romans, we read that the gospel of salvation had reached communities beyond the villages in Israel and was spreading throughout the world. The messengers were women and men who had experienced salvation through Jesus. The fruit of salvation is presented in the psalms as pure hearts from whom ethical behavior flows to others. God could have easily done everything faster as God working alone without humanity—Jesus could have appeared as an adult, teaching, healing, dying, and rising again. In three years he could have completed his mission and returned to God, but God chose instead to involve a village of people to work together to bring about the salvation destined for all of humanity.

What does this say to us today as we seek to bring Emmanuel into our lives and into the world that we live in? Salvation was born from a participatory process of working with others for the common good in changing the world. Similarly, our mission in the world requires conversations, the inclusion of all people who are involved in the issues that we seek to respond to. In a world where exclusion of the other and fear of the other is increasingly becoming the norm, we who follow Emmanuel are called to walk, live, and talk in a different way of conversation, working together, inclusively, in the struggle for a world where our hearts don't create separation but bring us together as a human family called together to respond to God's salvation.

CHRISTMAS SEASON

Nativity of the Lord

How are we laboring?

CHRISTINE SCHENK, CSJ

Isaiah 9:1–6
Psalm 96: 1–2, 2–3, 11–12, 13
Titus 2:11–14
Luke 2:1–14

> While they were there, the time came for her to have her child, and she gave birth to her firstborn son. She wrapped him in swaddling clothes and laid him in a manger. Because there was no room for them at the inn. —Luke 2:6–7

In reflecting on this beloved Christmas story, two things stand out for me. The first is the reality that the pregnant Mary and her husband Joseph had very little power or control over their own circumstances. What expectant parents would ever travel to a distant village, away from family and friends, when their firstborn child was due at any moment?

Only a family that had no choice but to comply with the demands of an oppressive, occupying government and a complicit religious leadership, both demanding exorbitant civil and temple taxes—despite the subsistence level standard of living for most in Palestine.

And then there is the matter of accommodations. No Holiday Inn here. No welcoming concierge. No room service—only a shelter for animals; only socially unacceptable shepherds (socially unacceptable because they smelled like the sheep they tended, possibly sheep the temple priests used for sacrifice).

The picture Luke paints is that of a low-income family on the margins of society, desperately seeking shelter so that Mary could labor and give birth protected from the elements.

I wonder how many refugee families from Syria, Iraq, Nigeria, or Yemen find themselves in similarly desperate circumstances this very night.

The second thing that stands out for me is how easily the Lukan author glides over the messy realities of labor and birth. We hear a lot about the politics requiring Joseph to register in his hometown, about the shepherds keeping watch, and about heavenly hosts of angels celebrating. All the good stuff. Of the actual birth we learn only the basics: It was time. The baby was born. We wrapped the baby in blankets. And that's pretty much it, folks.

If ever you wondered about who wrote Luke's Gospel, I think we can be pretty sure of one thing at least—this Gospel has to have been written by a man.

So tonight, since I'm the one who gets to reflect on this story, I want to fill in the picture and include some things a woman might remember if she were the one telling the story about a birth that changed the course of history.

As a nurse midwife myself, I've always been a little upset that no one ever includes the midwife in our Nativity scenes. We always find Mary, Joseph, baby Jesus, shepherds, angels and royal wisdom figures—we find donkeys, cows, sheep, sometimes Santa Claus and every so often a little drummer boy—but do we ever find a midwife? No! Why not?

No one seriously thinks that Joseph, as devoted as he was, actually delivered this baby, do we?

In first-century Palestine, it would have been inconceivable for a woman to give birth without the care and comfort of other women, and in particular the care of women the French call *sages-femmes*—wise women—the French word for midwives.

Even though Mary and Joseph were far from home, hospitality was pretty much the prime directive for the people of Palestine who were not far removed from their own desert wandering days. So I'm guessing the innkeeper, or more probably his wife, saw Mary's plight and sent for the wise women of Bethlehem to come and tend to her.

Since Mary was a first-time mom, there were no guarantees that she would emerge from her ordeal alive. Scholars estimate that maternal mortality rates were as high as 35 percent in the first century. Everyone would have known cousins, wives, sisters, aunties, and neighbors who had died in childbirth.

And while Mary and Joseph may have been more optimistic than most—given biblical accounts of the reassuring mystical experiences surrounding Mary's pregnancy—this would still have been a very scary time for both of them.

As a midwife telling the story, I'd surmise that Mary's labor probably began en route to Bethlehem. For first pregnancies, pre-labor with irregular contractions can easily last several days, with the regular contractions of latent—or early—labor lasting as long as twenty-two hours.

Christmas cards aside, we don't really know that Mary was riding a donkey; in fact, walking would have helped her labor progress. In Luke's story, Mary was probably well into her labor before finally finding shelter. When active labor arrived at last, surely the midwives had also arrived to help Mary manage her rapid, excruciatingly painful contractions and to show Joseph just how to support her as she began the arduous effort of pushing the newborn Jesus into a waiting world and, more immediately, into the midwives' waiting arms.

We won't dwell on Mary's anguished cries, her sweat, her blood, or her tears—but I can tell you that when that baby Jesus appeared at last, there was no need for chanting angels, because the joy and wonder reflected in Mary and Joseph's faces shone more brightly than any guiding star.

From a midwife's point of view, all that heavenly host stuff is afterglow.

The long-awaited child is born, Mary is safe, and Joseph is as proud and relieved as any new dad trying not to faint over the intensity of watching his wonder woman wife give birth.

Mary labored long and well to birth a child who would be all about God's love everlasting. When he was old enough, she would teach him the tenets of Judaism—summed up in her Magnificat hymn about a God who fills the hungry with good things and raises up the lowly.

Her boy-child would become a man of peace who would die a violent death even as he labored mightily himself to bring forth her Magnificat-God's justice-reign in the face of hatred.

My midwife's question for each of us tonight is to ask in what way are we laboring, like Mary, to birth God's abiding love into a world so much in need of it?

In what way are we, like Joseph, supporting the efforts of all who labor on behalf of the marginalized—refugees, immigrants, the homeless, poor, or victims of sex-trafficking?

In what way are we, like the midwives, supporting our powerful birthing God, who longs for right relationship and protection of a Mother Earth that, in fact, gave birth to us all?

To conclude, I share a prayer poem that pretty much sums up my midwife's understanding of the mystery, the challenge, and the hope of this most transcendent of nights:

Comfort, be comforted my people
for God's glad ecstasy
is new made flesh by human yes.

Through earth's long mourning
God waits again, near at hand
to birth the earth afresh
in celestial, millennial
unfolding of Christ's
transforming yes.
Yet, all depends
on a still small voice:
"Be it done in me . . .
as you would have it be."
Then God's glad life
now gifts, uplifts,
heals, enfolds,
newborn Christmas soul
In swaddling delight.
Come beloved Jesus,
herald now
God's just and kindly reign.
Teach us how
we learn to live
inside our God again.

      —C. Schenk 1999

Feast of the Holy Family

Caring for the anawim

CAMBRIA TORTORELLI

Sirach 3:2–6, 12–14
Psalm 128:1–2, 3, 4–5
Colossians 3:12–21
Matthew 2:13–15, 19–23

On this feast of the Holy Family, Matthew reminds us of the violence and persecution that families have always faced throughout history—even if you have a child who just happens to be the Son of God. From birth, Jesus's life is marked by the threat of violence, and it is the vindictive wrath of Herod which forces Joseph, Mary, and Jesus to seek asylum in Egypt. What we don't hear proclaimed in this reading are the three verses describing how Herod massacred every baby boy aged two and under in Bethlehem and its vicinity—a monstrous and appalling act of inhumanity by a despot of the ancient world.

Our modern world has more than its fair share of despots who too often turn their pitiless attention on children and families: maiming, murdering, bombing, gassing, raping, torturing, and trafficking them. Millions of Yemeni, Afghan, Salvadoran, Syrian, Kurdish, Honduran, Rohingya, and Guatemalan children, some alone and some with their families, are forced to flee unendurable conditions to find asylum in safe countries. Matthew's Gospel doesn't tell us how the Holy Family was received by the Egyptians, but it does tell us that they were able to remain in Egypt until it was safe for them to return to Nazareth. Tragically, in our modern times, it has become increasingly difficult for refugees and asylum seekers, children as well as adults, to find refuge in safe countries, including our own.

One of the beautiful legacies we have inherited from our Jewish ancestors in the faith is the concept of caring for and extending hospitality to the *anawim*. *Anawim* is a Hebrew word used to describe the poor and outcast, who have only God to turn to. In Jesus's time, like in our own, the *anawim* included the single mother; the orphaned, abused or abandoned child; the sick; the prisoner; and, of course, the immigrant and the asylum seeker. You just have to look at who Jesus ministered to in order to realize that he was steeped in this prophetic tradition of solidarity with the vulnerable and the marginalized.

We live in a society in which even our communities of faith are torn asunder by polarized views on how to respond to those who seek refuge within our borders. There are many in our families and workplaces, among our friends, and in our parishes, who have been made to believe that immigrants are to be feared and that they bring with them the very danger, lawlessness, and criminality that those seeking refuge here are trying to escape. It is heartbreaking to see how fear has replaced the abundant, welcoming, and inclusive love of Jesus Christ in some Christian hearts.

What is our collective responsibility in responding to the gospel call to care for the vulnerable and those on the margins, especially families and children, particularly when the response from the faithful can be so polarized?

What we have tried to do at my parish, Holy Family Church, is to make it possible for our parishioners to hear the stories of our recently immigrated brothers and sisters, and to connect with them in ways that encourage interaction and relationship. We have been blessed to have had a sister parish relationship with Dolores Mission in East Los Angeles for over two decades, which has allowed a two-way flow of grace between our parishes in so many ways and on so many levels. But it is the stories that have the most impact. Stories from DACA students who face deportation after living all their lives in Los Angeles open hearts by making their situations tangible. Stories from newly arrived families who were separated at the border under horrendous circumstances and are now trying to rebuild their lives put faces to what are otherwise statistics.

Building solidarity between communities that are very different, and yet have so much in common through our shared faith and humanity, is essential to making our hearts bigger and more understanding of one another's struggles. After all, it is through healthy, loving relationships that grace is unleashed in the world.

What we can often lose sight of is the need to build healthy, loving relationships with those right here in our midst who have viewpoints different from our own about immigrants and refugees, as well as about many other issues. Whatever our point of view, being harsh and judgmental about our differences creates an environment in which it can feel impossible to "put on love" and "allow the peace of Christ to control our hearts," as Paul urges us to do. But what a transformation takes place if we take to heart his message to the Colossians to "bear with one another in heartfelt compassion, kindness, humility, gentleness, and patience." If we start from this spiritual locus, stepping outside of our egos and need to be right, we are much more able to engage with one another in ways that encourage dialogue rather than acrimony.

As disciples of Christ, we are called to serve those in need and to advocate for justice on their behalf in a way that, to quote Benedictine Sister Joan Chittister, makes "the Word of God a blessing rather than a bludgeon." One of the hardest lessons of spiritual maturity is that souls and hearts change slowly. All the force in the world can't replace the power of dialogue and education to change a person's heart. Where better than in our parishes to learn the virtues and skills of living and growing together as a community of prophetic solidarity in the One Body of Jesus Christ?

Solemnity of Mary, Mother of God

Peace shaped by nonviolence, rooted in justice

MARIE DENNIS

Numbers 6:22–27
Psalm 67:2–3, 5, 6, 8
Galatians 4:4–7
Luke 2:16–21

When they saw this, they made known the message that had been told them about this child—that he, savior, Messiah, and Lord, would bring peace on earth, shalom, security, well-being. Woven into the fabric of Jesus's story from beginning to end is an identification of his mission with peace on earth—deep peace, peace rooted in justice, and a call to the task of peacemaking for those who would be disciples.

We say the words often and easily, don't we? "Peace be with you." We call him "Prince of Peace." We listen to the promise, "Blessed are the peacemakers, for they shall be called children of God." We struggle to follow his mandates: "Love your enemy," "Leave your gifts at the altar and go be reconciled with a brother or sister who has something against you." And we are deeply puzzled by his warning, "I come not to bring peace, but the sword." To seek peace, deep peace rooted in justice, shalom—not a mere absence of war, but the fullness of life for all—that is the Christian vocation.

Each year since 1967, on January 1st, the Solemnity of Mary, Mother of God, the Catholic Church has observed the World Day of Peace. In his message this year, 2017, for the fiftieth World Day of Peace, Pope Francis has asked Catholics to reflect on *Nonviolence: A Style of Politics for Peace.*

Nonviolence—a way of life, a positive and powerful force for social change, a process for ending violence without violence, for transforming conflict, and for protecting the vulnerable. Nonviolence.

A year or so ago, according to eyewitnesses, a group of Kenyan Muslims traveling on a bus ambushed by Islamist gunmen protected Christian passengers by refusing to be split into groups. They told the militants to kill them together or leave them alone. Some of the Muslim passengers gave non-Muslims headscarves to try to conceal their identities when the bus was stopped. One hundred passengers, mostly women, were on the bus at the time of the attack. Two people died, but the rest escaped.

Mobilizing courageous and creative people-power, nonviolence doesn't allow escape from conflict, but actively and powerfully engages and transforms it.

Last April, eighty-five people from around the world gathered for a conference in Rome on nonviolence and just peace at the invitation of the Pontifical Council for Justice and Peace, Pax Christi International, and other Catholic organizations. Many of the participants came from countries that have been at war or dealing with serious violence for decades: Iraq, Sri Lanka, Colombia, South Sudan, the Democratic Republic of the Congo, Afghanistan, Palestine, the Philippines. Their testimony was extremely powerful.

For example, Dominican Sister Nazek Matty, whose community was expelled from Mosul by ISIS, said, "We can't respond to violence with worse violence. In order to kill five violent men, we have to create ten violent men to kill them.

. . . It's like a dragon with seven heads. You cut one off and two others come up."

Many of the conference participants highlighted a deep yearning for just peace, especially in war zones around the world, and an amazing persistence in the pursuit of peace even in the most difficult circumstances. Courageous people in local communities living with unimaginable danger said, "Stop the militarization, stop bombing, stop the proliferation of weapons. Rely on nonviolent strategies to transform conflict."

The Church in Uganda, Colombia, South Sudan, and in many other countries has been involved in nonviolent peace-building strategies, engaging even the most violent actors in efforts to build a peace that is just and lasting.

Is there another path for the human community to take that will lead us beyond perpetual violence and war? What contribution could the institutional Catholic Church—all of us as a Catholic community—make to help the world find that other path and move in a direction that better reflects Jesus's teachings and way of life?

There is little doubt among scholars that the message of nonviolence is central to Jesus's life and teaching.

In his own times, rife with structural violence, Jesus proclaimed a new, nonviolent order rooted in the unconditional love of God. He called his disciples to love their enemies; to become peacemakers; to forgive and repent; and to be abundantly merciful. And he embodied nonviolence by actively resisting systemic dehumanization.

He defied the Sabbath laws to heal the man with the withered hand, confronted the powerful in the temple, challenged the men accusing a woman of adultery, and insisted over and over again that everyone has a place at the community's table.

Pope Benedict XVI said, "Love of one's enemy constitutes the nucleus of the 'Christian revolution.'" Every pope since John XXIII has spoken passionately about the futility of war and the urgent need to promote a peace that is just and lasting.

But, if we are going to make this Christian revolution real in the twenty-first century, nonviolence needs much more attention. There is never enough investment in the design of, or training in, effective nonviolent practices. Nonviolence is often misrepresented, misunderstood, or too narrowly defined. Nonviolence is not the same as pacifism, yet the terms are almost always used interchangeably, and nonviolence is much broader than civil resistance or protest.

What if Catholics were formed from the beginning of life to understand and appreciate the power of active nonviolence and the connection of nonviolence to the heart of the gospel—and were trained to understand the implications of "Love your enemy"? What if every Catholic in the world was alert to signs of impending violence wherever and at whatever scale—and was trained to help transform conflict?

What if the Catholic Church committed its vast spiritual, intellectual, and financial resources to developing a new moral framework and language for discerning ways to prevent violence and protect people and the planet in a dangerous world?

Now more than ever it is time to put active nonviolence—as a way of being, a method for change, and the foundation for a global culture of peace—into practice in our own neighborhoods and throughout the world.

Jesus proclaimed the reign of God as a new world of nonviolence where the dignity of every person would be honored and where justice and peace would flourish. Let us dedicate ourselves this year prayerfully and actively to becoming nonviolent people, a nonviolent Church, and a nonviolent world. Let us welcome the Prince of Peace. "Nothing is impossible if we turn to God in prayer," Pope Francis said this fall in Assisi. "Everyone can be an artisan of peace."

Epiphany of the Lord

A different way

Jane Wakahiu, LSOSF

Isaiah 60:1–6
Psalm 72:1–2, 7–8, 10–11, 12–13
Ephesians 3:2–3a, 5–6
Matthew 2:1–12

Happy feast of the Epiphany of our Lord! Today, we celebrate the revelation of the incarnate Son of God, Jesus Christ, to the world. Jesus was first revealed to the shepherds at the manger in Bethlehem, and now to the magi who came from the East to adore the newborn King. Imagine the conversations of the magi as they traveled to meet Jesus. Uncertainty and discovery marked their journey. Remember that there was no GPS to give them directions to where they were going. However, brightly visible light from a star was the compass on their journey to meet Jesus. In the first reading, the prophet Isaiah tells us that "the darkness covers the earth, and thick clouds cover the peoples." Light is needed to break the darkness—Jesus is the light. The vision and mission of God are evident in the incarnate Christ, the star, the true light of the world. As Isaiah points out, ". . . upon the Lord, the light shines, and nations shall walk by your light." In our reflection, I will focus on three themes: intention and motives, the meaning of the gifts from the magi, and a transformative encounter.

For me, the feast of Epiphany brings back memories of my childhood. When I was growing up in the countryside in Kenya, women (birthers) sang ululations announcing the birth of a baby to inform neighbors of a new member in the community. On receiving this news, women would fill baskets of presents with clothing and food for the baby and family. It was a joyful moment to introduce the newborn baby to the community. Like the magi, women waited with open hearts and minds in readiness to welcome the newborn into the community. Of course, the visit of the magi had a unique significance; they had been drawn by the Holy Spirit to seek the newborn Christ, "the true light which enlightens everyone."

On intentions and motives: Matthew's narrative is descriptive, telling us that the magi from the east arrived in Jerusalem inquiring about the location of the newborn king of the Jews, as they had seen a star rising and had come to pay him homage. On hearing this, Herod was perturbed and anxious about the questions the magi were asking. Consequently, he assembled the chief priests and scribes and inquired where the Christ was to be born. The response did not serve to ease Herod's anxiety, for he learned that, according to the prophet, the king was to be born "in Bethlehem of Judea." Herod asked the magi to return and let him know of the whereabouts of the newborn child. Of course, Herod's concerns were political and self-centered; his intention and motive were not to go and do homage to newborn Christ, but to harm baby Jesus and thus remove a perceived threat to himself.

Herod's action is not new in human interactions. Think about the active tensions or wars around the world, within nations, in communities and families. In conflict situations, we have suspicion, mistrust, and fear. We judge and are not open to alternative interpretations. Herod's experience is not far from our own, particularly in situations where answers do not favor our ideas or perceptions. When confronted by individuals with different perceptions than our own, let us learn to pause, to listen to our inner voices, and to check our motives and intentions before we respond.

On the gifts: The magi brought with them the gifts of gold, frankincense, and myrrh. These were meaningful and symbolic gifts. The precious and expensive gift of gold demonstrated the importance of Jesus, the savior of the world. Frankincense, a sweet perfume, often burned in the temple to worship God and was a sign that Jesus should be worshiped. Myrrh was used to keep things fresh, and to preserve bodies after death. Myrrh is a gift that would be used by the women to anoint Jesus's body when he dies. Indeed, the three gifts represented the mystery of the incarnation and foretold Jesus's suffering and death—completing the history of salvation.

On a transforming encounter: The encounter with Jesus was a life-transforming event for the magi. It was the culmination of a long physical journey that changed the course of their lives. Think of a memorable experience that has had significance in your life. These moments are rare and far between, but they remain vivid and clear in our memories. A single event can bring complete transformation of a person's life forever. Matthew explains that, after adoring Jesus, the magi "returned to their own country by a different way." The word "way" has several meanings, "*a course traveled, a new direction, a possible decision or outcome, a habitual manner, or a mode or pattern of behaving.*" Of course, the magi did not wish to inform Herod of where the baby Jesus was, but more significant and powerful was their encounter with Jesus: an encounter that so transformed their inner selves that they could not return to their old ways because through the Spirit, the one true mystery of creation, Jesus Christ, had been revealed to them.

Indeed, something deeper and extraordinary took place in their lives. The magi embraced a new way of life after their encounter with Jesus. Their new path and behavior were noticeable to others—a new direction in life. We are invited to pause and ponder: Do our encounters with Christ in the scriptures and the Eucharist transform our lives? Are we going to remain the same after these encounters? Let us look within and around our neighborhoods: Are there things we have taken for granted—the migrants, refugees, or people experiencing homelessness? We are called to step out of our comfort zones to visit, to be present, to accompany, and to provide for those in need. Pope Francis asks us to move to the periphery. We have a choice to remain the same or to open our hearts, to open our eyes to see the light of Christ in others, to walk with those who are searching, to purify our motives and intentions, for the Spirit is generous in guiding and accompanying us on our journey of life. God bless you!

Baptism of the Lord

Baptism: calling us out of our comfort zone

JANE M. CRUTHIRDS

Isaiah 42:1–4, 6–7
Psalm 29:1–2, 3–4, 3, 9–10
Acts 10:34–38
Matthew 3:13–17

A story of radical kinship: one who was ordained as *"a voice of one crying out in the desert, 'Prepare the way of the Lord, make straight his paths'"* (Isa 40:3, Matt 3:3), and the One who was born into human history to reconcile creation and restore peace. Today's readings remind us of who we are created to be and how we are to set out into the world. They also give us an example of how Jesus calls each of us to serve in an extraordinary capacity.

The baptism of Jesus is our baptism. It is the calling forth of a servant with whom God is well pleased and in whom the Spirit rests (Isa 42:1). Let us not forget that God is well pleased with each one of us and the Spirit is with us! Jesus's baptism marked his entry into public ministry, a radical ministry of compassion for the marginalized and imprisoned. A ministry of truth and healing with a message of peace. A ministry that was attacked and subverted by the most learned of religious leaders. A radical ministry that has spanned the test of the ages, giving us hope to persevere through challenges and celebrate the joys of our lives while we continue to love and be loved by those whom we encounter.

As I prayed with these readings, I was struck in a particular way by the interaction between John the Baptist and Jesus. That day, on the Jordan River, the missions of two cousins met in a seemingly extraordinary request, baptism for our Lord and Savior Jesus Christ. John, stunned, asks, "*Why are you coming to me?*" He knew his passion and purpose was to "prepare the way" for Jesus. I can imagine that this request from Jesus felt daunting. I wonder if John felt inadequate to complete the task. When I put myself into this story, I imagine my reaction would be to say, "That's above my pay grade" or "Not my job." This is usually my initial reaction when I'm out of my comfort zone or when the path I had envisioned has drastically changed. It's my way of relinquishing responsibility to those whom I think are better positioned for the task at hand.

Was this to be the day that John's mission ended and Jesus's began? I don't think so! Jesus's request invites John into a new purpose. He says to John, "*Thus it is fitting for us to fulfill all righteousness*" (Matt 3:15). Jesus's invitation pointed to John's innate holiness and ability to serve God. It recognized John's role in preparing the way and called John into service with Christ.

In 2013, at three and a half years of age, my son began having seizures. He had a great personality, although he was strong-willed, and was developing right along with his preschool cohort. Within days of his seizures starting and his beginning to take medicines to control them, his life and mine changed drastically. He stopped meeting age-appropriate developmental milestones and his behavior became combative and impulsive. Later that year Duncan was diagnosed with autism spectrum disorder in addition to epilepsy. I started relinquishing my responsibilities as a mother to doctors and therapists. I thought there was no way that I could be enough for my son. I was WAY out of my league! As time went on, I began to trust that I knew what was best for Duncan since I knew him best. This newfound confidence helped me guide discussions with his support network and become an active part of his learning and growing. I reclaimed my "first teacher" role.

When reflecting on the last number of years, in the context of John and Jesus's relationship, I realize that all of Duncan's doctors, therapists, teachers, and my support network accompanied us as we forged a new path. I did not give up being Duncan's mom; in fact I took on the role of advocate. I was being called to a radical and challenging new journey with my son. Jesus invited me to work with him to grow in holiness and cultivate Duncan's holiness. Christ has presented me opportunities daily to recognize my own worth and abilities while creating space for Duncan to become an independent, funny, and smart young man. While there have been many successes since his initial diagnosis, there have also been difficulties and lessons in humility.

It is for this purpose that Jesus instituted the sacrament of baptism. The gospel calls us to live a life that will challenge us and push us out of our comfort zones. At our baptism, we are claimed by Christ and restored to the holiness which reflects God's image. We are given the graces we need to follow Jesus and are anointed into service with him. With faith, we step forward each day to do important work that might very well be above our pay grade. However, we do so with the knowledge that God has "*called [each of us] for the victory of justice . . . as a light for the nations, to open the eyes of the blind to bring out prisoners from confinement, and from the dungeon, those who live in darkness*" (Isa 42:6–7).

Today we celebrate Jesus's baptism and the beginning of his public ministry. Let us also take time to contemplate our own baptism and recommit to living our baptismal call daily. As we work for justice in our own way, let our immediacy of action keep Christ's radical message of truth smoldering in our hearts and the hearts of those we meet.

My dear sisters and brothers, my prayer for you today is a humble knowledge of your own dignity as you work for justice, and a recognition of the gift of dignity that you give to others by your love. Amen.

LENT

Ash Wednesday

A communal commitment

SIMONE CAMPBELL, SSS

Joel 2:12–18
Psalm 51:3–4, 5–6ab, 12–13, 14 ,17
2 Corinthians 5:20—6:2
Matthew 6:1–6, 16–18

Hi. I'm Sister Simone Campbell, and I'm the executive director of NETWORK, a national Catholic social justice lobby here in Washington DC, and I want to share with you thoughts about Ash Wednesday.

I've always been puzzled about why we wear ashes on our forehead on Ash Wednesday, when the gospel reading for today clearly says, "When you fast do not look gloomy like the hypocrites, they neglect their appearance," and then the gospel says, "No, we should dress up, we should anoint our head, we should rejoice in public." Well, what I've realized is that wearing ashes on this day is like being at a rally. It's seeing all those who share this communal commitment to conversion during these six and a half weeks of Lent. It's like, as we say, wearing a button, and for us we wear buttons of Nuns on the Bus at rallies, and that's what the ashes on our forehead become on Ash Wednesday.

We know who stands with us and shares our commitment. It's that shared commitment—a communal commitment—that becomes critical for how we move forward together. Because Lent is not an individual action, it is communal, and in that communal action we have the hard work of being the Body of Christ, being engaged in our society. We know that when Christ was born—we celebrated Christmas not long ago—Christ as they say, "pitched his tent among us." And that same extension is what comes to us. We then have the responsibility of being God's body in our world—in a relationship—caring for those who are left out, caring for the marginalized, caring for the immigrant and the orphan, welcoming the stranger and the refugee, making sure that our faith values are extended. It's this one day of wearing our button, the sign that we're in this together with the ashes on our forehead, that we know we stand together in community.

And it is, as the first reading says, the "urgency of now." We need to gather the people, notify the congregation, assemble the elders, gather the children, the infants at the breast, the bridegroom, and the bride—all of us need to come together in the urgency of now. And, right now in our nation, from my perspective, it's never been more urgent that we together live our faith and respond to the call—the call to conversion. That is the hard work that is the urgency of now. So I urge you in this Lent to let your heart be broken open. Let us respond to the needs around us, recognize that as part of the Body of Christ we are called in this challenging time to live the asceticism of letting ourselves weep for our nation and then take action.

So then it will be, as Paul says in the second reading, truly an acceptable time, a time when we hear the Lord's call to the day of salvation. He closes by saying, "Behold now is a very acceptable time, behold now is the day of salvation."

Join me, I need you—and quite frankly you need me—to work together to create this day of salvation so that all are welcome. And "We the People" in our nation and around the globe will know the fullness of the message of Jesus, "All are welcome, all are together, all live in dignity."

We can do it, I know we can. Let's make this Lent about the communal act of conversion. Thank you.

First Sunday of Lent

Repentance that flows from love and mercy

DIANNE BERGANT, CSA

Genesis 2:7–9; 3:1–7
Psalm 51:3–4, 5–6, 12–13, 17
Romans 5:12–19
Matthew 4:1–11

Today we enter the season of Lent. While this season has traditionally been known as one of repentance and penance, the liturgical readings for the Sundays of Lent suggest that the primary focus is the mercy of God in the face of human sinfulness. This is not to say that repentance is unimportant—it is. However, repentance should flow from the realization of God's steadfast love and mercy rather than from some debt we might think we owe God. Today's readings illustrate this.

The first reading, from Genesis, features several episodes: the creation of the first man; his placement in the garden; the creation of vegetation out of the same ground from which the man was made; the temptation of the woman; and the sin of both the man and the woman. Any one of these themes could be the focus of our reflection. However, the passage from Matthew's Gospel describes the temptation of Jesus, suggesting that the prominent theme to be considered is temptation.

In the first reading, the snake engages the woman in conversation. Why her and not the man? This feature of the story has been variously interpreted. Some maintain that it is because women are less astute and more inclined to succumb to clever conniving, a misogynistic reading that has no grounding in the biblical text itself. Others counter this bias with a reversed sexist interpretation, casting the woman as the first theologian discussing the mysterious ways of God.

The choice of the woman reflects the strong wisdom character of the story. Various features allude to this. First, the snake is described as being "the most cunning of all the wild animals," an allusion to wisdom. Second, the discussion concerns the tree of the knowledge of good and evil, clearly a wisdom theme. Third, the dynamic within this discussion is one of decision, an activity that reflects wisdom. Finally, in the wisdom tradition itself, wisdom is personified as a woman (see Prov 1, 7–9; Wis 1, 6–10; Sir 24). Various reasons have been advanced explaining why wisdom was personified as a woman. The most commonly accepted explanation is that the ancient Israelites, or their ancestors, once revered a goddess of wisdom. While this is most likely true, it simply begs the question: Why female? Probably because wisdom was the treasure most desired by this people, and it is reasonable that in a male-centered society, what was most treasured would be personified as a woman. Thus, the choice of the woman rather than the man is in keeping with this particular biblical tradition.

Like temptation itself, the exchange between the snake and the woman is more subtle than it is direct, and she is caught in its subtlety. He never really lies to her. He tells her that if she and her husband eat, their eyes will be opened and they will know good from evil. That is exactly what happens. However, as is often the case with temptation, what happens is not what was expected, and it is only afterwards that they realize that they have made the wrong choice.

The temptation of Jesus is quite different. His tempter is direct, not subtle. In the face of temptation, Jesus makes the correct decision. While the first woman and man desired to be like God, attempting to grasp wisdom in a manner contrary to God's will, Jesus decided not to succumb to the temptation to use inappropriately the power that was his. In the wisdom tradition, options are placed before us, along with a glimpse into the consequences of deciding in favor of one or the other. The choice is ours to make. It is up to us to decide if the choice will be wise or foolish.

Perhaps it is the psalm response that sets the tone for today's reflection:

> *Have mercy on me, God,*
> *in accord with your merciful love;*
> *In your abundant compassion,*
> *blot out my transgressions.*
> —Ps 51:3

This opening verse contains two technical covenant terms: merciful or steadfast love (*ḥesed*) and compassion (*raḥămîn*). *Ḥesed* is the kind of love that insists: 'There is nothing you can do that will make me stop loving you.' *Raḥămîn* comes from the word for "womb" suggesting womb-love, a strong feminine image underscoring the intimate love a woman has for the child of her womb. This love and this compassion are characteristics of God's attachment to us; they do not refer to any sentiment we might have toward God. The psalm verse reminds us that the love and mercy of God are incomprehensible.

It is right that we begin our Lenten reflections with an acknowledgment of our propensity to yield to temptation, for without this acknowledgment we would not realize our need for God's graciousness. However, the Sunday readings prompt us to concentrate during this season less on our weaknesses and more on God's steadfast love and mercy.

Second Sunday of Lent

Seeing Jesus in a new light

LAURIE JURECKI

Genesis 12:1–4A
Psalm 33:4–5, 18–19, 20, 22
2 Tmothy 1:8b–10
Matthew 17:1–9

This week, I moved into a new home. The one I'm leaving has been my home for longer than any other in my life. I learned to be a single parent there. I got my younger boys through high school there, which was an adventure in itself. I learned to live alone there. And quite a few years ago, when my youngest son Joe moved home to help me after a surgery I was having, I learned how to live with an adult child. And when he married, I learned how to live with and form a brand new family with a loving daughter-in-law there as well. It's been a great place—a great life. But lately there's been another learning as well. And that learning is that as I approach my sixty-fifth birthday and get older, the steep, winding staircase in that house will not be my friend for long. And that one bathroom on the second floor will not suffice for the long term either.

This first place of independence has been my refuge and resting place. But I realize that it cannot be so forever—

mostly because of its structure. So over the past couple of years I have begun to look at this wonderful home in a brand new light. My reading of the story of the Transfiguration is about how the disciples got to see Jesus in a new light too. It sparked some thoughts connected with the events of my move, thoughts that became the center of my reflection.

First, they walked up a high mountain. I think that since it was noted that the mountain was high, perhaps it wasn't one of their usual places. I imagine that it wasn't such an easy climb. I imagine that the disciples wondered what was in store for them when they got to the top. Jesus had called them from their lives to follow him, and so far, so good. They had witnessed the feeding of multitudes. They had witnessed healings and raisings from the dead. They had heard teaching that both supported what they knew about being godly people and also turned the world upside-down with Jesus's focus on the poor, the marginalized, and the outcast. What might this mountaintop experience be for them? They didn't know.

How many times in our lives are we forced to go up a mountain? We all face difficulties in life and we all step into the unknown too. Sometimes just when we think that things are going well or turning around, we'll hit a bump in the road. Or—to continue with the mountain image—we encounter a crevice or a canyon that comes between us and our hopes and dreams. Sometimes it even comes between us and what we think God wants us to do. Sometimes it makes no sense. And yet we can't avoid the mountains. For me, this mountain had to do with facing one of life's transitions and continuing to take one step after another.

Second, Jesus took very specific friends up that mountain with him: Peter, James, and John. They were the same ones he took with him to Gethsemane. I was struck by the fact that even Jesus took his friends to share in this journey with him.

Even the son of God knew that the gospel could not survive without the people who most closely knew the story—the people who would still be here when he was no longer with them in the same way.

God—this Trinity of Persons—knows the value of relationship and reveals it to us. God revealed it to me in my meditation on this story. I cannot imagine pulling up roots after twenty-two years and moving out of my home without the support and love of a few very important people. The people who counseled and encouraged me were people who have been in my life a very long time (you know, the people around whom you might not be too embarrassed if they looked in the closet as you moved). Those are the people that go with you up those mountains. In the *way-too-many* moments of frustration during the process of moving it would have been way too easy to give up or to fall apart. But God put my family and my friends in front of me to keep calling me forward...and sometimes behind me to keep pushing me forward as well.

Third, the disciples were afraid when they got up there. When Peter, James, and John went up that mountain they most certainly didn't know what they were to encounter. They were afraid, as anyone would be. But they loved Jesus and they followed him, though they didn't really understand his true nature at that point. And now he was on a mountain in a bright light, talking to Moses and Elijah. What does one do with that? How does one process that experience? They had to be wondering what this would mean for their future.

I can't tell you how many times in the past months fear has grabbed onto me too in the process of buying my new home. Can I get a loan? Is this really the right decision? And just as with his friends on the mountain, Jesus knows how hard life is and how hard it is to follow. But he reaches out and touches them—as he touches us—with assurances that all will be well.

Finally, they had to come back down the mountain. Having had a glimpse of who Jesus is and having seen him in an entirely new light, they had to return to their ministry. They were changed. But was anything else?

I've never actually climbed a mountain, but I've seen one on TV. It's clear that—while it might not seem as hard going down as it is going up—there are real dangers in coming down the mountain too. There are still the canyons and crevices to deal with. You could slip and fall. You could lose your footing on a rock. You could get lost, because when you're up there among the rocks everything looks the same. And I also wonder if—in the going up and the going down— people might find it hard to breathe in that thinner air. I know that people have said to me many times in these past weeks, "Just breathe . . . just breathe."

For me, even though the truck is gone, I know the real work and adjustment is only beginning as I go down my mountain. I am wondering what life will be like and that's a little unsettling. I know as I go to work each day I look pretty much the same and work looks pretty much the same. But the transformation of my living has changed everything just as the Transfiguration changed everything for Peter, James, and John (and I might add for Jesus as well).

As we continue through this season of Lent, I think the possibility for transfiguration—for seeing Jesus in a brand new light—is open to all of us. We will go on with our lives as they were, but transformed. For the disciples that would mean a new perspective on the mission they accepted in following Jesus. In my case, it is a new place to live and a whole new way of living. And today and over the next days, as you reflect on this reading, I invite you to be open to the possibility of transformation, to be open to the gift of climbing that mountain with Jesus and seeing Jesus—and your life—in a brand new light.

Third Sunday of Lent

The woman who testified

MARY CATHERINE HILKERT, OP

Exodus 17:3–7
Psalm 95:1–2, 6–7, 8–9
Romans 5:1–2, 5–8
John 4:5–42 or John 4:5–15, 19b–26, 39a, 40–42

On this third Sunday of Lent, the Church throughout the world gathers with those who recently have begun a journey of Christian faith to reflect on the story of a woman whose encounter with Jesus was so powerful that many others from her home town began to believe "because of the word of the woman who testified."

We can all think of our own litany of those whose lives and words of wisdom have transformed our life journeys. For some, those wisdom figures are close to home. But at other times, the persons and encounters that transform our lives are quite surprising. Just recently, while watching the movie *Dead Man Walking* with a class here at Notre Dame, I was reminded that a man on death row was moved to confess his heinous crime and to seek forgiveness on the strength of the testimony of faith of another woman—Sr. Helen Prejean. At the same time, her words and witness moved a father whose son had been brutally murdered to turn to prayer and to struggle to forgive the man who had committed that unspeakable crime. On the strength of her testimony, and that of others who have joined with her, a country and a Church have been challenged to rethink and actively oppose the death penalty. The book and the movie *Dead Man Walking* are all the more powerful because they also reveal the human journey of Helen Prejean, the many encounters that led her to speak—and that enable her to continue to speak—her own word of testimony.

Today's gospel offers insight into the transformation of another missionary disciple, a woman who would have been on the margins of Jesus's world. Given the length of the narrative—almost the entirety of chapter 4 in John's Gospel—there is a real temptation to abridge the story. We worry that people don't have the attention span—or the time—to listen to the full story in a world where we communicate by tweets, instagrams, and snapchat. But when we cut out part of the story, we risk missing something crucial. In the shorter form of the gospel in today's lectionary, for example, we hear the good news that many Samaritans came to believe in Jesus, but the edited text omits what prompted that conversion by eliminating this line: "They began to believe in him because of the word of the woman who testified."

Maybe that crucial omission is enough to make us curious about the back-story of this missionary disciple. The Samaritan woman is the first of a series of women in the Gospel of John to proclaim the good news which they have seen and heard, a history of witness culminating in Mary Magdalene's testimony to her encounter with the risen Jesus: "I have seen the Lord."

The passage offered for our reflection today is an extended conversation that takes place between two strangers at the site of Jacob's well in Samaria at about noon, the time of day when there is the most heat, but also the most light. Jesus, a tired and thirsty itinerant preacher, has stopped to rest there on his long journey home to Galilee. As the scene opens, he encounters a woman who is going about her ordinary life, carrying out her daily domestic duty of coming to the village well to seek water, as do countless women around the world still today, if they are fortunate enough to have a reliable source of water.

Jesus initiates the extended conversation that follows, but it is the woman who asks the questions throughout the encounter. He asks her for the most basic of human gifts, the one without which we cannot survive: "Give me a drink." She is the one to ask the hard question, the "elephant in the room" so to speak: "How can you, a Jew, ask me, a Samaritan woman, for a drink?" She doesn't go into detail, but Jesus knows well the boundaries and hostilities that have come to separate the two descendants of Jacob who once shared a common heritage. By the time of Jesus, as the narrator reminds us, "Jews use nothing in common with Samaritans."

That could have been the end of the conversation—from both sides—but neither one backs away or refuses to engage. Jesus takes the woman and her question—her challenge—seriously. At the same time, he shifts the conversation away from traditional expectations and clear boundaries and speaks instead of gifts freely given, living water, and a spring welling up to eternal life. As the passage makes clear, however, we cannot recognize the abundant gifts offered by a stranger so long as we safely distance ourselves from that person as "the other."

Instead, Jesus speaks words of invitation, reframing the woman's challenge: If you knew the gift of God, and who is speaking to you, you would have been the one asking—for living water.

The woman's next question can be read at one level as if she has totally missed the point when she returns to concrete details: You do not even have a bucket, the well is deep. Once again, the conversation could have ended there. But her questioning is more profound than that, and Jesus hears her deeper searching, her real question: "Where then can you get this living water?" And her unspoken question: Who is this stranger who seems to be redefining religious traditions, but whose words and whose very presence speak to her at a deeper level? Jesus responds in exactly that deeper key: "Whoever drinks the water I shall give will never thirst . . . the water I shall give will become a spring of water welling up to eternal life."

The ambiguity about the woman's thirst—her true desire—continues. On one level she doesn't want to have to keep coming back to the well; but on a deeper level, like all initiates in faith, her response involves more than she realizes: "Sir, give me this water, so that I may not be thirsty." So finally they have switched roles in the drama: "If you knew the gift of God and who is asking you for a drink, you would have asked him and he would have given you living water."

However, the story doesn't end there in terms of the identity or mission of either one. The next exchange in the dialogue is often taken to be the dramatic center of the plot. Usually it is portrayed as some version of Jesus "calling out" the woman for her marital history of having five husbands and now living with another man. But the focus of the story is not on a sinful or loose woman, none of which is stated in the text, but rather on the deepening of this woman's faith, her growing desire for living water.

Just as Jesus could see her more deeply, so too she now sees him with more of faith's insight: "Sir, I can see that you are a prophet." She isn't afraid to pursue what that might mean, even to raise the long-disputed theological question between his people and hers—whether Mt. Gerizim or Mount Zion is the true sacred meeting place with God. Again, Jesus presents a new possibility: true worshipers will worship the Father in Spirit and truth; indeed such worshipers don't seek God; God seeks them.

That new vision prompts the Samaritan woman to affirm her hope for an anointed one to come—the Messiah, called the Christ—who will "tell us everything" by teaching as Moses did. Finally comes the real epiphany in the story as Jesus reveals to her what he has not yet said to any other disciple in this gospel: I AM. "I am he, the one who is speaking to you."

The chapter continues with an interruption from the male disciples, who have their doubts about what is going on, but, unlike the woman, they ask Jesus no questions. If we focus instead on the two thirsty pilgrims—the weary itinerant preacher and the woman whose faith tradition was considered suspect, it is clear that the dialogue between the two has revealed the true identity of each. Jesus gives no preaching commission to this new disciple, but he doesn't have to. Once the waters of Wisdom which she has longed for have welled up within her, she cannot keep from announcing what she has seen and heard. Like the other disciples, she leaves behind the life that she had known before, symbolized by her water jar—and returns to her own home town to announce the good news by inviting others to "come and see" and by raising another one of her powerful questions: "Could this man possibly be the Christ?"

Her encounter with Jesus, God's Wisdom made flesh, empowered her to become a missionary disciple, preacher of the good news which she herself has seen and heard. No wonder Pope Francis turned to her in his apostolic exhortation *The Joy of the Gospel* to remind all of the baptized, "in virtue of our baptism, all the members of the People of God have become missionary disciples (cf. Matt 28:19). . . . Anyone who has truly experienced God's saving love," the pope says, "does not need much time or lengthy training to go out and proclaim that love" (*Evangelii Gaudium*, #120).

Like the Samaritan woman, Pope Francis ends with a challenge framed as a question, one intended for all missionary disciples—women as well as men, young as well as old, newly initiated as well as long-time members of our communities: "So what are we waiting for?" (*Evangelii Gaudium*, #120).

Fourth Sunday of Lent

Seeing the world through God's eyes

RACHEL BUNDANG

1 Samuel 16:1b, 6–7, 10–13a
Psalm 23:1–3a, 3b–4, 5, 6
Ephesians 5:8–14
John 9:1–41

"It's always fun until somebody loses an eye."
That's what the adult in the room will often say to the kids
when playing around starts getting a little rough and rowdy
    and dangerous.

Never were truer words spoken.
(I know this is a cheeky way to begin a Lenten reflection,
but addressing a long gospel like this
halfway during a long season of repentance
merits at least a little bit of a lift!)

When I was in high school,
I was doing what big sisters do so well with little sisters:
pillow-fighting ... in the living room ... just before bedtime.
It was just supposed to be playful,
just a little mayhem, minimal destruction.

Then the corner of her pillowcase scratched my eyes,
and I could not see—literally.
I don't remember being in pain
as much as I remember being freaked out.
When I realized I couldn't see,
I started screaming bloody murder:
"You are SO dead! I'm gonna get you back for this!"

My sister was likewise freaked out,
terrified that she had blinded me,
and she was now crying tears of panic.
And since we lived in a very Catholic home,
she rounded up every rosary she could find
and began praying over me wildly
as I lay on the couch in darkness.
Imagine fistfuls of rosaries in a child's hands,
with the beads grazing over your face . . .
and sobbing, just crazy sobbing.
Meanwhile, my parents were in the kitchen
debating whether to take me to the emergency room.

Eventually, after what felt like forever,
my own fear subsided, and my vision began to clear.
My sight began to resolve and focus.

But honestly, I didn't say anything to my sister right away.
I let her continue her terrified praying and weeping,
trying to make deals with God if only I were healed.
    (So typical.)
I let everyone worry a while longer . . . because I wanted
    some payback.

Twisted? Yes.
Cruel? Yes.
Delicious? In the moment, yes.

All this is just to tell the story, not excuse the behavior.
There was, on my part, the temporary physical blindness,
coupled with a temporary emotional blindness.
And *of course* I'm sorry for aggravating the worry and
    anguish.
"Sin first, ask for forgiveness later," as that other saying
    goes.
(So much for Catholic logic and truisms.)

I hope that small, everyday life story
is one that you were able to see in your mind's eye and
    imagine as a short film.
Today's readings are likewise cinematic in their telling,
and they all play with notions of blindness and sight, dark-
    ness and light.

Samuel is out searching for the next king of Israel,
and God presents him, at last,
with a candidate he doesn't expect.
David, at first glance, doesn't strike him as the kingly type.
He's a shepherd boy—emphasis on boy.
But as with so many other stories in the Bible,
God chooses the one that we as humans always deem "least
    likely to _____ "—
the imperfect or unusual vessel—
to elevate and to do the hard work:
    Jacob, the younger twin;
    Moses, the stuttering murderer;
    Ruth, the foreign widow;
    Mary, the pregnant teenage mom;
    Jesus, the carpenter's son from the backwater of Galilee;
    Paul, the zealous convert.

We hear God gently reminding Samuel, who is scrutinizing
    one of David's other brothers first,

"Do not judge from his appearance or from his
        lofty stature,
because I have rejected him.
Not as man sees does God see,
because man sees the appearance
but the LORD looks into the heart."

As we look at ourselves now, if we were to see with the eyes
    of God—
perhaps with equal parts generosity and judgment—
what would we see?
Are we living according to God's desire and vision for us?

The psalm, second reading, and gospel acclamation next all
    come together
to remind us to let ourselves be led.
We are to surrender and trust in God as our shepherd,
leading us through darkness and difficulty,
ultimately home to blessing.

Paul writes a word of encouragement to the Ephesians,
telling them to wake from darkness and sleep,
and to walk in the light, as their new faith calls them to do.

That light, John then reminds us in the preceding chapter of
    this gospel, is Jesus,
the light of the world, the lamp to our feet—
the way, the truth, and the life.
Jesus is here to teach us how to see as God sees—
or as close as we can approach that.

Lastly, with the gospel itself,
I want to highlight two lessons out of so many possible
    ones.

The first one is this:
sometimes we suffer inexplicably, through no fault of our
    own
and surely not because of any sin or generational curse.
We are challenged to make sense of our own experiences.
Neither the blind man nor his parents are at fault, and yet he
    was blind his whole life,
until Jesus touched him and changed his life with this mira-
    cle of healing.
Disease, illness, and difference
need not be marks of bad character or signs of moral defi-
    ciency.
Rather, pain and suffering are part of normal life,
and thus they offer moments that call us to recognize God
    present and working in our lives
even though that may not seem possible,
even though that may not make sense at first pass.
Seeing the world through God's eyes—
with grace, mercy, and spiritual generosity—
can be difficult,
and we can only hope to grow with greater ease in that
through time and prayer and practice.

Walk in the light.

The other lesson to take from this gospel is
Jesus's lack of concern for the Pharisees' being upset with
    him.
They're upset because he broke the law forbidding work on
    the Sabbath.
Healing is *work*.
Just ask any caregiver.
But to channel a favorite movie, *When Harry Met Sally*,
why should goodness and justice—and love—wait?

In the final scene, on New Year's Eve, 1980-something,
Harry realizes that he's fallen in love with Sally,
and he's racing through the streets of Manhattan to find her
at a big, dumb dance with a boring date she'd rather ditch
    anyway.
And he breathlessly tells her,
"I came here tonight,
because when you realize you want to spend the rest of your
    life with somebody,
you want the rest of your life to start as soon as possible."
God can spark us, just like that.

Having light in our lives and seeing as God sees—
these are matters of great urgency.
If we can bring light to others,
shouldn't we do that without delay?
If we can bring life and help each other flourish and live in
    fullness,
shouldn't we do that without hesitation?
We can be light for one another now.
God is light for us now.
Live now.

Walk in the light.

Fifth Sunday of Lent

Do we recognize Jesus weeping with us?

KRISTA CHINCHILLA-PATZKE

Ezekiel 37:12–14
Psalm 130:1–2, 3–4, 5–6, 7–8
Romans 8:8–11
John 11:1–45

When I was in college, I participated in an immersion experience to Kingston, Jamaica. Our group consisted of twelve students and staff from the United States. As a part of the immersion experience, our campus minister always encouraged us to "participate, not anticipate throughout the day," so we really were not sure of what each day would hold for us. One morning, we piled into our trusty (though crammed) white, twelve-passenger car. Peter, our fearless Jamaican leader, drove us to our destination. We immediately rolled down our windows and the warm Jamaican breeze kind of kept us cool.

The scenery drastically changed as we traveled farther away from the former convent where we were staying for the week. The roads became more uneven. Crumpled wrappers, napkins, plastic bottles, and other pieces of trash littered the streets. Thin, stray dogs breathed heavily as they lay on the sidewalks, too hot to move. Children chased each other through alleys, their tummies poking out of their too-small shirts as their bare feet smacked the hot pavement. Adults sat, finding a bit of refuge in the shade provided by discolored buildings covered in faded graffiti, and they watched us as we drove by. The poverty was startling and it shook me.

This was not my first encounter with poverty: I had spent the majority of my time in college learning about problematic social structures, oppression, and "band-aid" attempts to fix deep-seated issues. Poverty manifested itself differently in my then-home of Los Angeles, but as we zipped through Kingston, I could picture injustices like the seemingly endless rows of tents on Skid Row.

I found myself uttering a phrase that echoed Martha and Mary's lamentation to Jesus in today's gospel: "Lord, if you had been here..." the scene we just drove past would look different (John 11:21). Out of the depths I cried to the Lord, "Hear my voice! Let your ears be attentive to my voice in supplication" (Ps 130:2).

My prayer was interrupted as we arrived at our destination for the morning: one of Saint Teresa of Calcutta's missions. We walked into a large, baby-blue room filled with plastic folding tables and matching baby-blue chairs. Elderly women living in the home sat in most of the chairs and hushed conversations could be heard throughout the room. One of the Jamaican volunteers ushered us in to join the women. I sat down next to Ms. Virginia, a 103-year-old woman, and we made polite and kind of awkward conversation. I wondered what I could possibly share with someone who had been on the earth for 103 years.

Not long after we sat down, another Jamaican volunteer skipped into the room with bowls of sliced oranges as she exclaimed, "Let's sing songs to Jesus!" The elderly women clapped and cheered. Ms. Virginia grabbed my hand and I noticed her hot pink nail polish. She helped me clap along to their songs of praise to God. Ms. Virginia's soft lips kissed the back of my hand and raised it high above her head. We laughed as we snacked on cold, juicy oranges, and Ms. Virginia shared pieces of her story with me—stories of abandonment and hardship, perseverance and faith. When it was time to go, she wrapped her thin, frail arms around me. "Thank you for being here today. I love you," she told me with glistening eyes and a toothless grin.

I felt deeply unsettled as we drove back through the uneven roads to the former convent.

Since that time, in the unrelenting fight for justice, I sometimes find myself wondering, "Lord, if only you had been here . . ." and it's easy for me to stop there. But the next part of this gospel passage holds so much guidance for us. That day in Kingston, Jamaica, Ms. Virginia and my community of twelve companions walked with me as I began to unpack that next part of today's passage: "When Jesus saw Mary weeping and the Jews who had come with her weeping," he was moved and deeply troubled (John 11:33). "And Jesus wept" (John 11:35).

So, from Martha, Mary, and their grieving community, we learn to ask a few important questions. First, do we recognize Jesus weeping with us? From there, where do we take that grief? We are called to be the hands and feet of Christ, so when we cry out, "Lord, if only you had been here . . . ," well, is he not already present within us, calling us to act?

Now, we must reflect on what that action might be.

After weeping with the community, Jesus went to Lazarus's tomb and he "cried out in a loud voice, 'Lazarus, come out!' The dead man came out, tied hand and foot with burial bands, and his face was wrapped in a cloth. So Jesus said to them, 'Untie him and let him go'" (John 11:43).

After Jesus weeps with us, we must ask ourselves how Jesus is crying out to us. "My dear, beloved friend, come out! Untie yourself." What do we need to do to untie ourselves?

What is it that keeps us bound? Maybe it's a fear of the unknown or maybe it's the thought of leaving our comfort zone; maybe it's something else entirely. Once we liberate ourselves, we can then ask ourselves how we will accompany and advocate for those who are tied up in suffering.

"Thus says the Lord God: O my people, I will open your graves and have you rise from them. . . . I will put my spirit in you that you may live" (Ez 37:12, 14). Let us pray for the compassion to weep with our communities and for the strength to accompany each other out of the tomb.

HOLY WEEK

Palm Sunday

Waiting with our suffering God

M. SHAWN COPELAND

Isaiah 50:4–7
Psalm 22:8–9, 17–18, 19–20, 23–24
Phil 2:6–11
Matthew 26:14—27:66 or Matthew 27:11–54

With Palm Sunday comes the week that Christians cherish as no other. We name it as Holy. With Palm Sunday comes the high solemn feast of God's dark glory and grandeur. With Palm Sunday comes the most awesome and terrifying time in the church year.

With Palm Sunday, we Christians take up again our peculiar waiting. We are accustomed to waiting; indeed, Advent creates in us an expectation—pregnant with life and possibility. During Advent, we wait in transparent joy even as we grieve over our scarred and battered world, our sinful human condition. The bright glory of the advent of our God enfolds us and our world in grace so that we might live in hope. But the waiting that begins with Palm Sunday is not the waiting of Advent. It is a peculiar, fearful kind of waiting and anxiety. In his passion, in allowing himself to be handled and seized, beaten and mocked and spit upon, Jesus discloses for us a distinctive quality of God which disturbs us: Jesus discloses the vulnerability of God, the willingness of God to suffer with us and for us. And even though we know the end of his story, the idea, the image of a suffering God disturbs and unsettles us.

We experience little or no difficulty with the child Jesus—after all, we were children and many of us are parents or god-parents or guardians to children. We learn slowly not to be dismayed by crying, we accept the 2:00 am feeding, we have memorized the quickest route to playing fields. Our children are miracles full of so much wonder and possibility. But images of the passion of Jesus disturb us.

Prior to the Second Vatican Council, Roman Catholic artistic representation of the passion of Jesus was often so graphic as to be gruesome and repulsive, but since the Council, we have beautified and sanitized the cross. For some time now, I have thought the old depictions preferable. For more than two hundred years, Christians were mocked and jeered by their colleagues, friends, and relatives because these men and women worshiped a God who had been crucified. And in their world (what we call the ancient world), crucifixion was the most scandalous and ignominious way to die. How, their colleagues, friends, and relatives wondered, could such sane and reasonable people worship a God who allowed himself to be crucified? This is the image of Jesus that unsettles us and disturbs us: a suffering God, a God who in free initiative gives the divine self over to suffering; Jesus, who in free initiative gives himself over to be handled and beaten, spit upon and tortured, crucified. This image unsettles us because it brings us to anguish: If our God so suffers, is so exposed to the brutality and power of the world, what shall become of us? It is a daring and daunting theological prospect—for God and for us. For as we believe that our God suffers—we who confess, who worship, who love, are called to a share in the suffering of Jesus, a share in the suffering of the peoples of our world. Moreover, we who confess, who worship, who love, are charged to bring about with him and with them that trajectory of expectation released at the advent of our God, signified in the Resurrection, and to be realized in the eschatological banquet.

With Palm Sunday comes the high solemn feast of God's dark glory and grandeur. Now begins the most awesome and terrifying time in the church year. Now begins our vigil; we wait, we stand beside and with our God who loves us and suffers with us, beside us, for us. But we can stand with our God only insofar as we stand beside and wait in active and compassionate solidarity with children, women, and men who suffer concretely, unbeautifully, and actually in our world that is God's world—the poor, the oppressed, and the excluded; abused children, battered women, and homeless men; those who believe, those who believe differently, and those who are afraid to believe. We stand and wait in love for Love to cast upon us the rays of dark, divine glory.

Holy Thursday

*Hearing and responding to God's call
to serve people*

Virginia Saldanha

*Exodus 12:1–8, 11–14
Psalm 116:12–13, 15–16bc, 17–18
1 Corinthians 11:23–26
John 13:1–15*

When she was ten, an Indian nun, Sr. Jyoti, was inspired to live as a missionary among the poorest in India. With difficulty, her family let her go to join the Salesian Missionaries of Mary Immaculate. She was there for just about two years when she felt that being in a convent was not what she had dreamed of, so she left to become qualified as a nurse and midwife. During her internship, she would go to nearby villages and work among the poor. However, she realized that it was not easy or safe for a single woman in India to go out alone in the evenings when it was growing dark. She decided to go back to the convent where she made her final vows. But she grew restless with institutional life. She struggled to get the convent authorities to yield to her request to be sent to work among the poorest people. After some time, her request was granted and she finally went to live and work among India's poorest and most exploited lower-caste people.

Friends, this brief account of Sr. Jyoti's struggle to respond to the call of God in servant leadership encapsulates the message I would like to highlight today—"hearing and responding to the call of God to serve people." In the first reading, God calls Moses and Aaron to lead the people of Israel out of their slavery in Egypt.

The second and gospel readings narrate how Jesus, before submitting to his final sacrifice in answering God's call, gave us a model for service in answer to that call. Jesus demonstrated for his disciples what leadership truly means when he, their Master, stooped down to wash their feet. He showed us that true leadership in the Church is "SERVANT LEADERSHIP"! He said, "I have given you a model to follow, so that as I have done for you, you should also do."

When he broke the bread and shared the wine that symbolized his body broken and blood shed for standing with the poor and the outcast and questioning the injustices of his time, he called upon all the disciples at the table to do the same in memory of his sacrifice. The disciples included women who would have been present at the Passover meal, as they are even today in Jewish households. But somewhere down the line in Catholic tradition women were edited out.

Jesus's sacrifice is celebrated in the liturgy of the Eucharist, which is highly ritualized today. Holy Thursday celebrates the institution of the Eucharist. It is also a day of celebration of the priesthood of Jesus, and by association all priests (who traditionally are all male). Many of us women feel strongly our exclusion from responding to the stirring within us to answer God's call to serve people through ordained ministry.

Jesus did not institute a priesthood, he did not give names to ministries within the community. The Pauline churches seem to have been charismatic communities operating under Paul, without any clearly structured organization. Ministry belonged to all, for each member had a charism (Rom 12:4–8).

Jesus asked his followers only to do what he had done. Jesus handed his disciples the legacy of a challenging servant-hood. It involves humility in service and sacrifice even to the extent of breaking one's body and shedding one's blood.

Holy Thursday places before us the challenges involved in following Jesus's model of service among the People of God.

Women are living this model of priesthood, and are being true to their baptismal anointing as "priest, prophet and leader." In various milieus, where you may not find a sacra-mentally ordained priest, many women around the world are living the priesthood of Jesus in servant leadership, being the presence of Jesus to people. The women in Amazonia are doing this! Sisters in India live and work among the indige-nous and poor people of India, and in fact two sisters lost their lives standing for the rights of their people. Women show the least and the last the loving and compassionate face of God. Women live their priesthood where they are planted, and demonstrate to the sacramentally ordained ministers what the priesthood of Jesus truly means.

Let us all, dedicated women and men, continue to live our priesthood in our communities, neighborhoods, and societies as God calls us, and to create a non-clerical and non-hierarchi-cal church as Pope Francis urges us to do in *Querida Amazo-nia*. We only need courage to think local and impact the global Church.

Good Friday

What do we do with so great a love?

JOAN S. DAWBER, SC

Isaiah 52:13—53:12
Psalm 31:2, 6, 12–13, 15–16, 17, 25
Heb 4:14–16; 5:7–9
John 18:1—19:42

There is a song that invites me into Good Friday. It is called "Open My Eyes" by Jesse Manibusan. The refrain that captures me is:

> *Open my eyes Lord, help me to see your face,*
> *Open my ears Lord, help me to hear your voice,*
> *Open my heart Lord, help me to love like you.*

To love like you . . .

It is Good Friday. What do we see . . . whom do we hear . . . who calls us to love? Good Friday is a day of remembering and entering once again, with each other, into the deep mystery of God. We want to bring ourselves just as we are—with all our pain and our sinfulness, our love, our longing and our deep gratitude. We want to be with each other, to be opened to see the great love God has for us.

I work with survivors of human trafficking. They are women who have been betrayed, physically and mentally

81

abused, stripped of their humanity, tortured, isolated, and abandoned. Listen to what they say to us: "I am here in plain sight and yet I am invisible to you. I felt like no one cared—I just felt invisible." Wendy said, "I was crying out for help but I didn't believe anyone cared or could hear what was happening to me." Jen said, "I have no love in my life, I don't know what love is—my trafficker manipulated me, used and abused me. I need to learn to love again."

In the first reading we see one who was spurned and avoided by people . . . one from whom people hid their faces, and turned their backs, and closed their eyes. They didn't want to see this suffering servant of God. In the gospel, we see this suffering in all its depth and rawness, we see the betrayal of Jesus by Judas, by Peter, and by the crowd, the people Jesus interacted with daily. While they knew Jesus, they were deaf to him, to his teaching, to his voice and the way he taught them to love. Jesus's way of loving was just too hard, too challenging, this selfless, forgiving, merciful love.

As we open ourselves to see, hear, and love, might we be able to recognize that merciful forgiving love in our own lives, in our family, in our neighbors, in our country, and in our world?

We know, at times, the sinfulness we see in our world is just so hard to bear and blocks us from seeing with the eyes of love. My work with women survivors of human trafficking helps me to recognize what this lack of love looks like close to home. You may have your own examples: the immigrant families left languishing at the borders, an abusive spouse, abuse of our vulnerable earth home, immigrant children held in cages. We see and are so aware in these examples of the absence of love. Sin indeed is the absence of love.

In a world that seems so filled with selfishness, hatred, violence, cruelty, death, destruction, and total disregard for life, life in any form—how do we experience this selfless love? I have seen it in the sisters who opened their home and said yes to bringing women survivors of human trafficking to live with them. They didn't put their own lives and routines first; they let that go and allowed themselves to be changed by the women survivors they lived with and accompanied. We may also know this love in those who genuinely and selflessly love us: in our friends, family, community; in role models like Gandhi, Dorothy Day, Martin Luther King. We too have been given the potential for this kind of loving. It is in each and all of us if only we can see and recognize it.

It is such great love to give your life for another, and isn't this exactly what Jesus does, and did all through his life, selflessly giving himself away for the sake of the other? Isn't this what Jesus invites us to? Jesus became one of us—he came to be with us and walk with us, to accompany us in all the messiness and suffering of being a human person. I find that such a great consolation—to know God is with me, with us now and always. God has given me and given us God's own life in Jesus: a life filled with forgiving, merciful love. So great a love!

Good Friday is clearly about deep, faithful, steadfast, merciful love. Jesus shows us how to love, to love like God. Jesus's whole life and ministry and death show us how to love. The question is, "What do we do with so great a love?"

EASTER SEASON

Easter Sunday

The women who did not lose hope

MARGARET A. FARLEY

Acts 10:34a, 37–43
Psalm 118:1–2, 16–17, 22–23
Colossians 3:1–4
John 20:1–9

Today is the feast of Easter. We do not celebrate this feast as if it were only a past event. It is intimately related to our own present lives. It is the center of our hope, the mandate of our proclamation, the source of our joy even in the midst of our sorrows. We hear in our hearts, and we say again and again to one another: "Jesus is risen as he said. Alleluia! He lives and is with us still. Let us rejoice and be glad." We ourselves experience dying and living in the unending life of God, in the forever present life of Jesus, and in our deep inklings and hopes of the meaning of resurrection.

This year on Easter day, of all the treasures in the many biblical passages that precede and follow the Resurrection of Jesus, the Church has given us (in its lectionary) a particular text to ponder, a text from the gospel attributed to John. It tells us the story of Mary of Magdala coming to the burial place of Jesus. She sees that the stone has been removed from the tomb. Immediately, she runs to find Peter and another disciple, bringing them to see the situation. They come, they may begin to believe, and then they return home. She herself, however, remains weeping next to the tomb.

If we look ahead to similar texts unfolding in Eastertide, we note that Mary Magdalene appears in every one of the four Gospels, always searching for the body of Jesus. And except for the version in John's Gospel, other women join her in this task and longing. Altogether, it becomes clear that it is these women who go first, before anyone else, in the early morning, to bring spices and to reverence the body of Jesus. In every telling of this, similar elements in the drama are repeated. The message is conveyed to Mary Magdalene that Jesus is not there, and that he has risen from the dead. The women are moved (or commanded) to go quickly to tell the disciples that the body of Jesus is gone, and that he is alive. Sometimes in this story the disciples run to the tomb, sometimes they are skeptical—they respond to the women in unbelief, rejecting what they say as "pure nonsense" (Luke 24:11; Mark 16:11). In Matthew's rendering, Jesus himself comes to meet the women, greeting them, allowing them to worship him (Matt 28:9). In each description, the women respond in powerful ways: fear, weeping, joy, yearning for an even greater sense of Jesus's ongoing presence. The role and responses of these women cannot be underestimated if we seek to understand the meaning of resurrection—Jesus's resurrection and our own.

But let us return to Mary Magdalene, weeping outside the tomb (John 20:11–17). Angels ask her, "Woman, why are you weeping?" She answers, "They have taken away my Lord." Then she turns around and sees Jesus, but does not recognize him (we know the story well). Jesus says to her, "Why are you weeping? Whom are you looking for?" She still does not recognize him. He calls her name, "Mary," and she beholds him. For Mary Magdalene, tears of joy supplant tears of loss, but neither are wholly behind her. She experiences wondrous fulfillment of her search, but also nonfulfillment when, in the midst of her utter joy at beholding the risen Christ, she hears the loving words, "Do not cling to me." What can this mean?

Imagine the transformation of her grief into joy when she hears her name and beholds the one she seeks. Yet in that very experience of joy is the paradoxical requirement of what might be called a "discipline of nonfulfillment." "Do not hold on to me," Jesus says. In this is the essence of what we know as the "already" but "not yet" of our existence. "Do not hold on to me, because I have not yet ascended to the Father" (John 20:16–17).

We have learned something about sorrow and weeping—from Jesus and from Mary Magdalene. There are different kinds of tears—tears of desolation which, if they have all been shed, leave the well dry. But there are also tears that water our hearts and give us strength and peace in real union with Jesus Christ. These are tears that turn us not in upon ourselves, but open us to union with God and our brothers and sisters. Such tears may even move us to action on behalf of God's reign and the welfare of our neighbors near and far.

God, we believe, is present everywhere, charging the world with grandeur, hovering over it and dwelling in it, groaning within it for life and glory. Jesus, the one who emptied himself in order to gather us into himself; who made our world his home and did not abandon it, now transforms (or aims to transform) our hearts and our world, holding us into what is promised—what is not yet full, but is somehow already here. Jesus himself rejoices in his Resurrection, and he shares his joy with us. Why? Because the joy of Jesus is *for us*—no less than his suffering, no less than his labor, no less than his death. *Everything*, if we can only receive it, is for us and for all creation: his love, his incarnation, his divinity, his truth, his pain, his glory, his Spirit, his life in time and eternity.

The women who came to find Jesus did not scoff, did not disbelieve, did not lose hope—and they found him before any others did. It was they who first spread the amazing news that has brightened our world ever since—whether in sorrow or in joy. Like these women, we, too, believe and speak in our hearts and voices: "Jesus is risen as he said. Alleluia! He lives and is with us still. Let us rejoice and be glad." Everything is new. It is time for us to Arise and meet the new dawn.

Second Sunday of Easter

The visible wounds of Christ

JEANNIE MASTERSON, CSJ

Acts 2:42–47
Psalm 118:2–4, 13–15, 22–24
1 Peter 1:3–9
John 20:19–31

All of us have our stories. The best ones rarely are about times when everything went smoothly—no, we tell stories about mistakes and crises, about clumsiness and human error. And everybody tells the story from his or her own perspective, so that often we wonder whether the tellers were all at the same place at the same time! This Gospel is no different. Matthew tells only of the resurrected Christ meeting the Eleven on the mountain, where all doubted. Mark's story is that Jesus appears to "the eleven" at table and rebukes *all* of them for their lack of faith. Luke's story has the two disciples who met Jesus on the road to Emmaus return to the apostles in Jerusalem, where Jesus appears to all thirteen—all of whom were terrified. In all accounts, Jesus says, "Peace be with you." Only in John are there locked doors. Only in John is Thomas missing, necessitating a second appearance.

And only in John did Jesus give the ten the Holy Spirit and send them out—what were they doing still behind locked doors a week later?

On many levels, the details don't matter—the point is that the resurrected Jesus returned to his friends, bringing peace and reassurance and commissioning. At the same time, the details give us insight into the humanness of the followers. Even in Gospel times, vulnerability wasn't highly rated.

One detail to notice in every account is that the resurrected Jesus has visible wounds. Resurrection comes at a price. It always follows the cross; it carries indelible marks. Resurrection does not negate suffering. Suffering is part of every story.

We who have been baptized into the one Body of Christ are constantly being shown the wounds of Christ. We are witnesses to horrible atrocities against all of creation: our waters and mountains, our forests and plains, our human brothers and sisters around the globe. Some are blatant; others more subtle. War and poverty, racism and greed, human-induced climate change, selfishness and egotism, human trafficking and various phobias, sixty-five million displaced persons around the globe, and so much more. All these stories invite us back into the atmosphere of today's first reading from Acts: how are we believers pooling our possessions—our faith, our strength, our leadership, our influence, our relationships—to assure that all have what they need? Such concern for one another is apparently as counter-cultural in much of our world today as it was for the early Christians.

We have much to learn about discipleship. We have much to learn about loving one another as God has loved us. We have much to learn about being one human community, one creation of a loving God who longs for unity. With us, as with Thomas, Jesus the Christ has infinite patience and mercy, waiting for us, as for Thomas, to choose: belief or disbelief. No pressure, only opportunity. No seduction, only invitation. No fear, only peace.

We are invited into resurrection, over and over again. How is our story different because we know we have been redeemed? Resurrection, if we truly open ourselves to it, makes us more truly the selves God created us to be: open, inclusive, generous, loving.

We don't have two thousand years of tradition to give us answers to current crises. We have only faith and one another. How will our story of discipleship be told to future generations?

Peace be with you. Love one another—ALL of one another. Go out and make our resurrected God visible!

Third Sunday of Easter

Coming into the fullness of His glory

Anita P. Baird, DHM

Acts 2:14, 22–33
Psalm 16:1–2, 5, 7–8, 9–10, 11
1 Peter 1:17–21
Luke 24:13–35

As we continue to celebrate the greatest event in the history of humanity, the scriptures proclaim repeatedly—just in case the reality of this astonishing truth is too much for us to comprehend—that this Jesus, this Jesus, born into poverty, who lived in an obscure village called Nazareth, whose parentage was suspect, who died on a garbage heap on the outskirts of town, one among many criminals—that this Jesus died and rose according to God's preordained plan for our salvation.

God has raised him from the dead and he now sits at the right hand of the Creator in glory.

Easter ushers in the hope and promise of new life. After the cold and dark of winter, the sun now shines brightly on our brittle bones, giving them new life.

What was perceived as dead was only asleep, and the greatest testimony to this miracle of faith is that if a barren tree can produce new life, surely, we will live for all eternity in his love. Death for once and for all has been conquered. "Death, O death, where is thy sting"?

Through the power of the Holy Spirit, Peter and the other apostles, released from the chains of fear, could stand boldly in the synagogue and on the streets of Jerusalem and proclaim that this Jesus, who was crucified by the authorities, through the power of God has the last word, for he is the Word made flesh—The Logos of God.

It is this Jesus, the Logos of God and the risen Lord, whom the disciples meet on the road to Emmaus.

Let's imagine the conversation between the two friends as they traveled to Emmaus.

"What really happened?" says the first disciple. "We witnessed his condemnation, his beating, his crucifixion and death. He was cold and very much dead when they placed him in his mother's arms . . . when they laid him in the tomb that Nicodemus provided."

"We felt totally abandoned as we scurried and hid for fear that we would be next. What had his life been all about? Why did we leave everything to follow him only to have it end on a hill at Calvary? Surely, God did not mean for it to end this way."

"How do we make sense of the senseless? Were we duped? Made fools of?"

"Now some women want us to believe that his body is no longer in the tomb."

"How are we expected to wrap our minds around all that has happened?"

And yet, as in the case of these two disciples, it is when we are most vulnerable, most afraid, and most doubtful that Jesus is revealed.

We can only imagine that the faith of these two very close friends of Jesus, who knew him intimately, had been shaken to the core. Life had thrown too many curves their way. Sometimes, life can become too much for us to cope with. Why did God allow my child to die before she had a chance to experience life? Why is my body ravaged with cancer? Why have I lost all that I worked for—my home, my job, and my savings? Why has God forsaken me?

It is precisely in such moments that Jesus draws near. He will never, ever leave us alone. He is our lean-to post. He is the best GPS one can have on this journey.

The scriptures tell us that "Jesus himself drew near and walked with them but their eyes were prevented from recognizing him."

How often have we failed to recognize him in the forgiveness of a friend, the hug of a child, a physician's healing touch?

How many times in our self-absorption or pity-party have we been prevented from recognizing him?

And when he asks them, "What were you discussing?" they become incredulous at the insanity of the question. "Are you the only visitor to Jerusalem who does not know of the things that have taken place? Where have you been?"

Yet Jesus responds not defensively, but with a question. "What things?"

Jesus never imposes. He knows that it is important that they be allowed to speak to the burning questions lodged in their hearts. We must be free to seek God if we are to ever find the God inside of us.

He knows that they will never recognize him if they are not able to speak their truth, to drop the blinders of doubt from their hearts, to trust in the goodness of God even when it is not easily visible.

He invites them to speak from their hearts and they do. They speak of their hope that Jesus would be the one to redeem Israel, only to see him die a shameful death.

It is only after they speak their truth that he admonishes them and reminds them that, as faithful sons of the Torah, as his followers, they should understand what the prophets have written and that, in understanding, their eyes would be opened. They would understand that he was destined to suffer and die, for as sin entered the world through one man—Adam—one man had to suffer and die to save the world.

We know that his words, his teachings, set their hearts on fire because they invited him to stay with them. Once we have met the savior, we want to remain in his presence, to have him stay with us.

It took only a simple invitation. They did not have to beg or apologize. They simply had to ask and he stayed with them. Jesus always waits for the invitation.

And in the breaking of the bread, their eyes were opened and they recognized that this stranger in their midst was their Lord and Master.

That is the power of the Eucharist. In the breaking of what looks like a simple piece of bread, we become aware of who we really are as members of his one body. Those who celebrate this mystery become a new creation. Just like the disciples on the road to Emmaus, our eyes are opened to our oneness with all of humanity, to pain and suffering, to the cry of the poor, the migrant, the immigrant, women, children, people of color, the sick and elderly, the imprisoned.

In the breaking of the bread our eyes are opened; we recognize the risen Christ. But this Christ does not stay. He vanishes from our sight, leaving us with the burning desire in our hearts to be Christ in a world that is crying out for healing.

The gospel tells us that they did not stay in Emmaus but rather got up and returned to Jerusalem. They knew where they needed to be and what they needed to do. They returned to bear witness that in the breaking of the bread we are one with all of humanity. I am my brother's keeper. I am my sister's keeper. I am my brother and sister.

A powerful image of the breaking of the bread for me is a mural of the Last Supper by Samuel Akainyah, which is painted on the chapel wall at Saint Sabina Church in Chicago.

Around the table are men, women, and children from every tribe and nation (some famous and others not), and in the center is a very faint image of Jesus. When the mural was being painted, I asked the pastor, Father Michael Pfleger, why the image of Jesus was so faint. The answer I received from Father Pfleger is what I believe is at the heart of this encounter on the road to Emmaus in the breaking of the bread; what I believe is at the heart of our Christian faith as Easter people, people whose hearts are burning at the recognition of the Savior.

I believe it is why the disciples immediately returned to Jerusalem and why we are sent each and every day to bear witness to the power of the risen Christ in our Jerusalem communities and throughout the world.

"*Until everyone is welcome at the table, Jesus cannot come into the fullness of his glory.*"

As disciples of Christ, it is our baptismal and eucharistic responsibility to bring Jesus into the fullness of his glory by standing in solidarity with a sister or brother who is struggling to reclaim his or her human dignity; by working to chip away at the walls of division and hatred; by bearing witness in the breaking of the bread that at the banquet of the Lord there is no room for hatred or division. We are all God's children— Jew, Christian, Muslim, Sikh, Hindu, Buddhist; black, white, brown, or yellow; male or female, gay or straight. All are welcome.

Stay with us, Lord, for we have seen you in the breaking of the bread, and our hearts are burning within us, for you have the words of everlasting life.

Fourth Sunday of Easter

Cultivating an attitude of silence

ANNE ARABOME, SSS

Acts 2:14a, 36–41
Psalm 23: 1–3a, 3b–4, 5, 6
1 Peter 2:20b–25
John 10:1–10

We live in a world afflicted by a cacophony of voices. We are bombarded by an avalanche of digital distractions—whether on social media or emails, on our iPads or iPhones, on our televisions or in our newspapers. Added to this digital chaos are other voices that compete for our attention or attempt to shape our image of ourselves and our world.

At times these voices become so loud they drown out our very capacity to think, to reflect, to stop and notice what is truly essential and what makes us truly human. At other times, such noise and distraction create confusion and intensify our inability to act. We ask: What, in a world where there seems to be no end to a string of bad news, can I do? Floods, droughts, conflict, sectarian violence, people on the move confronted by walls of xenophobia and bigotry. . . . The list is as frightening as the noise it generates is deafening.

Today's gospel, as told by John, invites us to notice and listen to one more voice. It is the voice of the Shepherd who says: "My sheep hear my voice"; "I am the Shepherd who calls my own sheep by name and leads them out.... My sheep follow me, because they recognize my voice." This voice is refreshingly different: the voice of the Shepherd does not assail us with material distractions; rather, the Shepherd offers us life: "I have come that you may have life in abundance." What a consoling voice amidst the chaos and confusion of our twenty-first-century digitalized world! The voice of the Shepherd restores our inner peace and calm. The Shepherd's voice refocuses our attention on that which is truly life-giving.

But there is one condition for hearing the voice of this good and life-giving Shepherd. The word is SILENCE.... Silence is not merely the absence of noise. Silence is our capacity for depth and interiority. Silence takes us to the place where true encounter happens between us and the Shepherd who calls our souls out to green and verdant pastures. I recall a poem by Harry Alfred Wiggett; he says,

> Silence is
> sitting still
> standing still
> lying still
> consciously
> gratefully
> gracefully
> breathing...

This is the kind of silence that enabled Elijah to hear God's small, still voice; the silence that empowered Samuel to say to God, "Speak, I hear you, I am listening"; it is the silence that Psalm 46 invites us to: "Be still and know that I am God; be still and know; be still... be."

I hear in today's gospel an invitation to cultivate an attitude of silence. This attitude of silence begins when we stop and listen—like Elijah on the mountain, like Samuel in the temple, like Hannah at prayer, and like Mary at the Annunciation. It doesn't take much; it could involve as little as retreating from the digital chaos that surrounds me—just for a few minutes, even a couple of minutes, at a time. It means trying to find our own Interior Castle where the confusion and chaos of "thieves and robbers" give way to the consoling and comforting voice of the Good Shepherd. Cultivating silence and creating a space of silence where God encounters us freely takes effort, but it's one step at a time, one day at a time. Think of it: how much richer our lives would be if we could only intersperse our frenetic busyness with little pockets of silence!

Something else about silence: there is a powerful and empowering quality to the gift of silence. Years ago, I read a story in Chinua Achebe's classic, *Things Fall Apart*, about a Mother Kite who sent her daughter to bring back food. When Daughter Kite brought back a duckling, Mother Kite asked: "What did the mother of this duckling say when you swooped in and carried its child away?" "It said nothing," replied the young kite. "It just walked away." "Then, you must return the duckling," said Mother Kite. "There is something ominous behind the silence." And so Daughter Kite returned the duckling and took a chick instead. "What did the mother of this chick do?" asked the old kite. "It cried and raved and cursed me," said the young kite. Mother Kite replied: "There is nothing to fear from someone who shouts."

As a woman, I am deeply in tune with my inner capacity for thought, reflection, and action. As an African woman Catholic, I have heard the voice of the Good Shepherd calling me by name, emboldening my imagination, and strengthening my resolve to strive for fullness of life for me, for my sisters, and for my brothers. Yet I am too painfully aware, also, that my voice may not always be as loud, strident, and valued as those who shout with power and authority, those who lord it over others in the Church.

Nevertheless, life-giving and empowering voices of women are rising across the world, in church and society. We have heard the voice of the Good Shepherd; we have been nourished by God's gift of abundant life. With passion and compassion, we lift our voices to ask: Why is our Church not listening to us? Why does our Church not hear our voices?

Like the Good Shepherd, we bring gifts of life to renew our broken world. We come with our talents and gifts to nourish the community of the risen Christ. We come not to burgle or to steal, but to cradle humanity with compassion and to reveal the face of God as love. Let me leave you with a quote from the second African Synod: "Women in Africa make a great contribution to the family, to society and to the Church by their many talents and unique gifts.... The Church and society need women to take their full place in the world 'so that the human race can live in the world without completely losing its humanity'" (*Africae Munus*, #55).

As women, our voices are an embodiment of this quest for humanity promised us by the Good Shepherd.

Fifth Sunday of Easter

Seeing ourselves as prophets

DONNA L. CIANGIO, OP

Acts 6:1–7
Psalm 33:1–2, 4–5, 18–19
1 Peter 2:4–9
John 14:1–12

On this fifth Sunday of Easter, we hear rich words that should gladden our hearts and fill us with energy for the gospel mission of Jesus!

The two lines from the gospel that jump out at me are:

Where I am you also may be, and
Whoever believes in me will do the work I do.

I recently heard a lovely story of a small boy who fills his backpack with Twinkies and juice boxes and prepares to leave the house. His mom says, "Where are you going?"

The boy answers, "I am going to find God." So off he goes.

He ends up in a local park and sits on a bench next to a homeless woman. He takes out a Twinkie and a juice box and starts to unwrap them. The woman watches and smiles at him and he laughs and offers her a Twinkie and a juice box. They both eat, talk, laugh, and enjoy each other. Soon the boy says goodbye and sets off for home. The woman leaves and goes off to find her friends. When the boy gets home his mother asks, "Did you find God?" He says enthusiastically, "Yes, and God is a woman!" The homeless woman meets up with her friends and says, "I met God in the park today—and he is a little boy!"

The story is an illustration of the two lines in today's gospel that struck me: "Where I am you also may be" and "Whoever believes in me will do the work that I do." Both the boy and the woman manifested God where they were, in what they were doing, and in how they related to each other.

Each of these phrases is essential for us. We bring Christ wherever we are. We are given the work to carry on the mission of Christ in our time and in various ways.

This is so clearly expressed in a poem prayer by Teresa of Avila:

> *Christ has no body now but yours.*
> *No hands, no feet on earth but yours.*
> *Yours are the eyes through which he looks compassion on*
> *   this world.*
> *Yours are the feet with which he walks to do good.*
> *Yours are the hands through which he blesses all the*
> *   world.*
> *Yours are the hands, yours are the feet,*
> *yours are the eyes, you are his body.*
> *Christ has no body now on earth but yours.*

On this fifth Sunday of Easter in the Eastern Church, the feast of Saint Photine is celebrated. Saint Photine is the name given to the Samaritan woman with whom Jesus spoke at the well. The name means "*luminous one*"—because she heard the words of Christ and recognized him as the savior.

We don't celebrate or name her in the Western Church. In one way we celebrate her as a critical person in the gospel, and in another way she is invisible. Yet, this woman is a major evangelizer and a prophet. It is through her words and witness that a whole village comes to believe in the Christ of the living water.

Think of what you do each day to witness Christ to others. Think of the things you say and do to advance the mission of Jesus. Just like those in our first reading from Acts, "*we devote ourselves to prayer and to the ministry of the word*" to continue to spread the word of God and increase the number of the disciples in our families, our work, and our ministries.

We know that the women of scripture have played pivotal roles as prophets, preachers, evangelizers, deacons, and leaders of prayer and Christian communities.

Today we continue to have opportunities and obligations to step up and lead in those same roles. People so often tell me that they are grateful for the leadership of women in the Church and that they are eager to hear their voices more often.

As hard as it is, we need to seek those roles and see ourselves as prophets manifesting the Word of God to all. And we must help others do the same.

As Jesus said, "*Where I am you also may be*" and "*Whoever believes in me will do the work I do.*"

"*Christ has no body now on earth but yours.*" It is up to us! Amen.

I would like to leave you with two questions for reflection:

Who were the prophets you met this week who
   manifested God to you?
In what ways were you a prophet for others?

Sixth Sunday of Easter

Let's use our voices

Sarah Attwood Otto

Acts 8:5–8, 14–17
Psalm 66:1–3, 4–5, 6–7, 16, 20
1 Peter 3:15–18
John 14:15–21

My family moved to Austin, Texas, the summer before I started eighth grade. On that first day of school as I walked through the front doors, I felt pretty isolated from the different cliques gathered around their lockers, and the overwhelming fear in my mind was whether I'd have someone to eat lunch with that day. My only solace at that moment was singing, "Jesus loves me" over and over in my head as I walked down that hallway with trepidation. Somehow I knew, beneath all of my fears and insecurities, I was not alone. Jesus loved me and walked with me down the corridor of my new school.

I imagine the disciples felt similar fears and insecurities whenever Jesus mentioned his departure to them. He was their team captain! He was their teacher, their mentor, their friend. Without him, their mission would not exist. But in today's gospel we hear Jesus promise his disciples that his physical absence will be overcome by the never-ending presence of the Advocate, the Spirit of truth. *I will not leave you orphans, I will come to you.* You will not be alone as you enter new territories and encounter new situations.

God was with me on that first day of eighth grade. God was with me when I moved away from home for college. God was with me when I walked away from a long-term relationship in grad school. God was with my husband and me as we moved across the country, far from family and friends, in the first year of our marriage. God was with me in the long and lonely hours of laboring and delivering my first child. Are there lonely journeys that come to your mind from your own life? Walking into the hospital room of your child who has cancer, leading a line of cars in a funeral procession for your spouse. In all of those moments, God promised to be with us, and promises still: *I will not leave you orphans. I will come to you.*

And this promise is significant as we look at the first reading and hear about Philip sharing the good news of Christ in the city of Samaria. This was a new phase in Christ's mission, moving the gospel beyond Jerusalem and Judea to Samaria. At other points in the gospel, the Samaritans had rejected Christ, so I can imagine Philip felt a bit uneasy as he set out on his travels. But in today's reading, they were of *one accord* in paying attention to what Philip was saying and they accepted Christ. I love the line: *And there was great joy in that city.* I love the particularity of that. There was joy in that city, in the city of Samaria. Like Philip, we aid in the Spirit's bringing of joy to a particular city, or community, or person. Philip's fears—as well as our own—need not stop the efficacy of God's Spirit.

And joy is the foundational marker of Christian identity, isn't it? Today's psalm is bursting with joy, recounting the wondrous deeds God has done throughout salvation history. But we all know that a closer look at the psalms reveals that this joy is not a superficial emotion—there are some significant challenges in the life of faith, moments of fear and desolation.

Saint Paul in the second reading certainly reminds us of that. The life of faith is not immune to suffering. Christ *himself* suffered. But the continued gift of the Spirit's presence allows us to stay grounded and give an account of our hope even amidst suffering and fear, because we are not alone in our trial.

I love the old Quaker hymn, "How Can I Keep from Singing?" It so beautifully captures the reason for hope:

No storm can shake my inmost calm
while to that rock I'm clinging.
Since love is lord of heaven and earth,
how can I keep from singing?

I had not yet learned that song in eighth grade, but despite my fears of entering a brand new school, I could not keep from singing.

So what does it mean to accept the Advocate, the Spirit of truth? What's the implication of today's readings? We, too, are called to expand Jesus's mission as Philip did in Samaria. We're called to walk into new territories, brave challenging situations, and accompany those who may be different from us. But we do not do this alone: we have been given the gift of the Spirit who accompanies us and advocates for us in our mission. So how can our voices, then, be a gift for others?

The Spirit of truth demands that we stand in solidarity with those who are marginalized, persecuted, and forgotten and advocate on their behalf. The Spirit of truth demands bravery and boldness in the pursuit of justice. The Spirit of truth is very much alive in the margins of society, and in the messiness of our lives, demanding that no one be orphaned.

So as a Church, let's use our voices and not stop singing.

Solemnity of the Ascension
May we begin looking around

Teresa Maya, CCVI

Acts 1:1–11
Psalm 47:2–3, 6–7, 8–9
Ephesians 1:17–23
Matthew 28:16–20

We celebrate the feast of the Ascension today! As I reflected on the readings, I immediately imagined the disciples looking up, and even wondered if they tried to stop Jesus. And then, all the Easter stories of the weeks leading to this moment came to mind: Jesus appearing to the disciples, time after time, greeting them always by saying, "Peace," or "Do not be afraid." And yet here they are, those poor hard-headed disciples, after journeying with Jesus, after experiencing the power of the Resurrection, after learning that Life conquers death, here they are: "looking up."

How could this be? They had been comforted and taught by Jesus himself! Despite all the joy and wonder of those Resurrection days, here they are "looking up"! In fact, it takes yet another messenger to jolt them by asking: "*Why are you looking up at the sky?*"

So, I wonder about all of us. On this day, we too, stand with the disciples "looking up." Even after we have celebrated

Easter for one week after another, even after renewing our profession of faith in Jesus Christ, and even though most of us can witness to the transformation Christ's presence has meant in our lives, we need to ask ourselves: How many of us find ourselves, more often than not, just looking up?

How many of us, like the disciples, ask Jesus: "Are you at this time going to restore the kingdom to Israel?" How many times have we asked Jesus, "Please chime in, right about now!"

Of course, we look up! That is why Jesus's words to the disciples are also meant for us, for all of us—cloud-gazing followers: Trust, trust me, trust my words, trust my deeds, trust your experience of me. It's time to stop looking up and begin looking around!" The Book of Acts is very clear: "Wait for the promise of the Father about which you have heard me speak." Trust.

As we hear these words, something begins to shift, because we know that over and over, Jesus has offered us a gift—the gift of the Holy Spirit. With the disciples, we heard him say "Holy Spirit" many times: "The Holy Spirit will come, the Spirit will guide you, the Spirit will comfort you." . . . Spirit here and Spirit there. In fact, we say "Holy Spirit" all the time: when we bless ourselves, when we need guidance, and today we need to ask ourselves: Who is the Holy Spirit in our lives? Do we leave room for the Holy Spirit? Are we listening to the Holy Spirit? Do we trust the Spirit? The Letter to the Ephesians comforts us: "May the God of our Lord Jesus Christ give you a Spirit of wisdom and revelation, resulting in knowledge of him." We cannot trust on our own; we need the gift of the Spirit.

Today we need to hold on to this gift, this gift of the Spirit, that will enlighten us to an even deeper knowledge of Jesus the Christ, a knowledge of the absolute joy and transformation of the mystery of his Resurrection. With the Spirit, we will bring the experience of the Resurrection into our daily life. Only then will we become what Jesus hopes for us: authentic witnesses of the love that transforms all forms of death. Only then will our discipleship move us to teach what Jesus has taught us—that love can change everything: our hearts, our communities, our broken nations.

With this Resurrection faith, we can appreciate the "hope that belongs to our call." And what a hope it is! Not just for us as individuals but for our families, our communities, and our planet. Today we need to pray for the gift of the Holy Spirit, the Spirit that can flow among us, through us, that can inspire us, encourage us, that will transform our doubt into witness.

Filled with the Holy Spirit, we will be ready for mission. The Spirit will enable us to heed Jesus's call: "Go make disciples of all nations." Pope Francis would say, "Go forth, *en salida*, move—*andale*; go tell the good news of Jesus Christ, go speak about the love of the reign of God, go share the story about the world Jesus dreamed for us: a community of fellowship, forgiveness, inclusion, a place of mercy; go . . . teach, go do what I did; go wash feet, and forgive, and gather, and celebrate. Go forth to show the world that love has power over death!"

When we give the Spirit a chance, we will forget about looking up; we will begin looking around, we will turn to each other, we will collaborate and work for justice, and then we will hear Jesus whisper to us: "I am with you always, until the end of the age."

What could be more "awesome"? What could bring more joy to our hearts? What else could make us sing with Psalm 47 than to know that we are never, ever alone? Jesus the Christ is with us:

"I will be with you always, until the end of the age."

May our celebration of the feast of the Ascension open our hearts to the gift of the Spirit, so that we can witness to our experience of Jesus Christ.

May we trust his promise, his teaching, his presence among us, always, "until the end of the age."

And may we stop "looking up" and begin "looking around," as we go forth on the mission of building the reign of God! Amen!

Pentecost

Trusting the Holy Spirit to shape us

C. Vanessa White

Acts 2:1–11
Psalm 104:1, 24, 29–30, 31, 34
1 Corinthians 12:3b–7, 12–13
John 20:19–23

> *Spirit of the living God, fall fresh on me.*
> *Spirit of the living God, fall fresh on me.*
> *Melt me, mold me, fill me, use me.*
> *Spirit of the living God, fall fresh on me.*

In the African American religious experience, there are many spiritual songs and hymns that attest to the presence of the Holy Spirit in the lives of the community. Such songs as "Spirit of the Living God," "Every Time I Feel the Spirit," "I'm Gonna Move When the Spirit Say Move," and "There's a Sweet Spirit" describe the power and presence of the Holy Spirit to move and animate a community of faith as well as individual persons.

I am reminded of these songs as I read and pray with the Acts of the Apostles and in particular the Pentecost event described in Acts 2. You know, the Holy Spirit is so evident and present in the Acts of the Apostles that it could even be called the Gospel of the Holy Spirit, and I believe many scholars have done just that.

The Holy Spirit as described in the Acts of the Apostles is a living Spirit that moves the community from fear to fearlessness, from faltering to faith, from powerlessness to passionate power. The Spirit transformed individuals into an inclusive community that then became a missionary church. In many Christian churches today, it is the custom for members of the congregation to wear red to celebrate the Pentecost event, which the author whom we call Luke describes as tongues of fire. Even today many will still wear red in solidarity with one another during this time of physical and social distancing. We will be reminded that the Pentecost event was experienced by people of many races and ethnicities during difficult times.

> *Every time I feel the Spirit moving in my heart*
> *I shall pray*
> *Every time I feel the Spirit moving in my heart*
> *I shall pray*

As people of faith living during a time of the pandemic, we are called to pray and to listen to the Holy Spirit which will move us to the right action. We have seen how social media has been used to bring communities together in prayer and in song, to teach and preach through spiritual practices— such as global rosaries, novenas, contemplative practices, and virtual retreats. We have already seen during this time how communities and individuals have responded to the needs of the poor, the recently unemployed, the sick and our elders, our brothers and sisters. We have now begun to slow down and maybe even listen to the Spirit and respond to the needs of our communities. We are reminded in our second reading today in Paul's First Letter to the Corinthians that we are all one body, and that, through the power of the Holy Spirit, we are one and our gifts are to be used for one another.

I'm gonna move when the Spirit say move,
I'm gonna move when the Spirit say move,
When the Spirit say move, I'm gonna move oh Lord,
I'm gonna move when the Spirit say move.

In today's gospel, Jesus said, "as the Father has sent me, so I send you," and he breathed on them and said: "Receive the Holy Spirit." This Spirit moved them to let go of their fear and to be persons of mission.

In these days, we are so in need of that Spirit of fearlessness. Many are afraid of what is to come. As Jesus has reminded us again and again, do not worry, I am with you. We cannot predict the future, but we can allow ourselves to be open to receiving that sweet Holy Spirit that will give us what we need in the days ahead.

Saint Irenaeus of Lyons, one of the first theologians of the Christian Church, states that the Spirit came down with power to open the gates of life to all the nations and to make known to them the new covenant. He further writes that in baptism we have become one in body and through the Holy Spirit we become one in soul. These are powerful and transformative words. Do we truly believe that we are of one body and through the power of the Holy Spirit, one soul? How are we preparing to receive the Holy Spirit today?

Spirit of the living God, fall fresh on me.
Spirit of the living God, fall fresh on me.
Melt me, mold me, fill me, use me.
Spirit of the living God, fall fresh on me.

This song, *Spirit of the Living God*, ends with the invocation to ask the Spirit to melt me, mold me, fill me, use me. As people of faith, we must be open to trusting the Holy Spirit to shape us, fill us, and use us. Like those first disciples in the Upper Room, may we be open to the coming of the Holy Spirit during this time of pandemic to use us and transform us for the good of all.

Finally on this Pentecost, I leave you with the words of Servant of God, Sr. Thea Bowman:

> If you believe that the Spirit that lived in Jesus, that the Spirit that lived in the disciples, that the Spirit that moved in the early Church is the same Spirit you receive in your baptism and confirmation, say AMEN.

> If you believe that you, like Jesus are called by the Spirit to share the Spirit in the world, to call forth the giftedness of God's people, say AMEN.

> And if you believe that the Spirit of God is able to transform the water of your reality into purest wine, if you believe there is nothing God can't do, say AMEN, AMEN, AMEN.

Happy Pentecost.

ORDINARY TIME

Second Sunday in Ordinary Time

The saving power of innocence

DIANA CULBERTSON, OP

Isaiah 49:3, 5–6
Psalm 40:2, 4, 7–8, 8–9, 10
1 Corinthians 1:1–3
John 1:29–34

There is nothing more appealing than innocence. That is why we pass baby pictures around and why we love to watch children in the lap of Santa Claus. We treasure innocence because we know that it doesn't last. Soon our children will grow up, learn of danger, learn that they can be hurt, and discover that the world beyond them can be threatening. Is it possible to experience evil and violence and remain untouched? Is it possible to see or experience the depths of human hatred and not become cynical and distrusting? Can innocence survive?

At the beginning of John's Gospel, we hear of a preacher in the wilderness who calls his listeners to repentance, who offers a cleansing ritual for those who are less than innocent, a baptism that symbolizes a change of heart. And in the midst of his efforts, he sees someone approaching him. "Look," he declares. "Look at the Lamb of God." Translation: Look at the one person among us who does not need to repent—not a child, but an adult—well aware of the violence and criminality of others, and willing to live among us and change us. "Look," says John in the desert. "Look at the Lamb of God."

We know enough of the background of this text to remember that in the Exodus story, it was the blood of the lamb on doorposts that once saved the children of Israel from the Angel of Death. And we remember the Suffering Servant of the prophet Isaiah who was compared to a lamb led to the slaughter. And that the Crucifixion occurred as lambs were being slaughtered for the Passover feast. The scriptural reference to Jesus as the Lamb tells us something about the deep meaning of his life, of his crucifixion and how Christ saves us. Innocent of all charges, he responds to violence with prayer for his executioners. We who remember his death know that we are not innocent. We are in our own wilderness—and we need saving.

And so at every Mass Catholics are drawn into the presence of innocence when we say, "Lamb of God, you take away the sins the world, have mercy on us. Lamb of God, you take away the sins of the world, grant us peace." Jesus offers us mercy—and the peace for which we pray. The Crucifixion is our rejection of his first self-offering, but in spite of that rejection, he forgives—and calls to his Father to forgive. His innocence before the law and his love for his persecutors is our salvation.

The image of the Lamb of God reminds us that we are saved—not by pain but by love, by the love of Christ for his persecutors, by his forgiveness of all of us who are not very innocent and who may still believe that violence can expel evil—or what we perceive as evil. Our response to Christ's offer of forgiveness and shared love must be gratitude, sorrow for how we ourselves have been persecutors, and hope for an end to the violence of human beings to one another—not just in the Roman Empire when crucifixions were common, but in every place on earth where men and women must fear for their lives, where innocence is no protection against the violence of the powerful.

A significant feast is celebrated at the end of this week: the feast of another innocent—a young girl whose self-offering became famous in Christian history. According to the testimony of the early Church, she was murdered—presumably before a crowd—because she had dedicated her life to Christ—and resisted a forced marriage. Young women then—and perhaps even now—are not expected to resist cultural or political imperatives. Whatever the details of her martyrdom, she is one of the earliest of a long line of men and women who have died as witnesses to their fidelity to conscience. She was not the first—nor certainly the last—to resist persecution, not the first nor the last to be murdered by forces more politically powerful. She is the elder sister of the four church women murdered in El Salvador (working with the poor, they were considered subversive), of Sr. Dorothy Stang murdered because of her protests against the violation of the Amazon rain forest and the people dependent on it, of Sr. Mariam Vattalil of India, murdered because landlords were offended by her work with the landless poor, of the innocent in every land who have been brutalized by those whose are stronger—and who have different fidelities. These and all who give their lives to the work of the gospel are part of a long history of men and women whose innocence—like the innocence of Jesus—was no protection against the violence of those in power.

But strangely enough it is the blood of the innocent—not the violence of the strong—that saves us. Jesus is the Innocent One whose forgiveness gives us reason to hope and whose grace strengthens the weakest among us. Like John the Baptist, we can recognize him in our own wilderness and know that the violence of our world will never be the last word. The last word is mercy, for which we pray at every Eucharist—where we behold the Lamb of God who takes away the sins of the world and who continues to offer mercy to those who love him. John in his desert reminds his listeners: it is mercy that saves us, not political power, not military power, not our presumed sinlessness, not even our good works. There is only one who is innocent before God. And John calls us to see, to look at Him, to look at the face of mercy, to look to the One who alone can give us peace.

Third Sunday in Ordinary Time

We are children of the light

Jocelyn E. Collen

Isaiah 8:23—9:3
Psalm 27:1, 4, 13–14
1 Corinthians 1:10–13, 17
Matthew 4:12–23

The people who have walked in darkness have seen a great light!

A great light.

In the northern hemisphere where I live, we are right in the middle of the cold, dark winter. We live in a world wrecked with violence, fear, poverty, exploitation, human trafficking, starvation, greed, deception, mass incarceration, racism, sexism, malnourished children.... The list is seemingly endless. Yet, we are children of the light. We believe in this gospel of light and love that can transform us all into Resurrected people, freed from all fear and divisions, freed from all human limitations.

Ordinarily on Sunday mornings, I am breaking open our word of God with my incarcerated sisters and brothers in a prison. Prisons can be some of our darkest places. Yet I don't see the darkness, and I do not recall the darkness when I reflect on my visits. I see the light and the hope in the sisters and brothers that I pray with every week. I see a hope that abounds in the midst of incredible odds.

Perhaps the best example of hoping against hope is in my friend Chloe. I met her during a retreat I led with a group of women while I was in graduate school. I was so struck by her genuine joy and enthusiasm. When the retreat was over, Chloe came over to me to thank me for coming and for being a part of the retreat team. Then she invited me to return to the prison sometime soon to lead a retreat of my own design and she said, "Bring your friends." Chloe left me tongue-tied, which is not an easy feat. When the chaplain came over to me at the end of the evening, she said, "So what did you think about the retreat?" and I told her of Chloe's invitation. The chaplain just smiled and said, "You know, she's a lifer," and my jaw dropped. A lifer means that she is serving a life sentence.

I wondered how on earth Chloe could possibly remain so hopeful, so filled with life, and so welcoming to me. Chloe welcomed me to a place where she was trapped. For life. I cannot imagine how it feels to be locked up for the rest of my life. Chloe's invitation became a voice in my head and a prayer in my heart. I thought about her all the time. I felt as if Jesus were inviting me to follow him and return to that horrid, huge, dark state prison! I felt drawn to the light that was there in the darkness. I did return, just six short weeks later, to lead another retreat, with eight friends. And, because we believe in hope, in a God of love who never abandons us, there was a miracle that occurred for Chloe.

Chloe was granted parole in 2015 after serving twenty-one years . . . and Chloe was released from prison in May of 2016! She is working hard to support herself. She is filled with light and joy. Chloe learned how to spread light in absolute darkness. And now she continues to do so beyond the four prison walls.

In our gospel today, Jesus not only invites the apostles to drop everything—their nets, their boats, their fish, their families, and follow him, but he does so in a way that is so attractive that the apostles literally drop everything now and follow Jesus. How did Jesus say this? What exactly did he say? What would Jesus need to say to you to lead you to drop everything and follow him? How would you react if Jesus were standing in front of you right now?

Would you go with Jesus? He is the traveling healer walking all over the country meeting people that no one else wants to talk to. He roams the streets. Could you spend your life living in a tent like a migrant or a person who was unhoused to be with those on the margins? Do you know anyone who has done this? Do you know any missionaries and/or volunteers? What called them to do this?

If Jesus were here today, where would he live? Who might he talk to? Who might need his love the most?

I have had the privilege of spending time on the margins in shelters, assisted living homes, schools, orphanages, soup kitchens, detention centers, prisons, and communities that literally live in piles of garbage. These kinds of places really make me stop and wonder, "Why, God?" How can I have had enough good food to eat, a good education, a safe place to play, a roof over my head, clothing to wear, access to healthcare, a loving family, and technology to use, when so many millions of people on this planet never will? How can I preach the gospel when there are so many people waiting? Waiting for treatment, waiting for a job, waiting for a break, waiting for freedom.... Life can be miserable.

And yet!

We live in the light!

We are children of the light!

The Reverend Dr. Martin Luther King Jr. said, "Darkness cannot drive out darkness. Only light can do that."

Light doesn't have as much work to do to dispel darkness. The light just needs to shine even the tiniest of tiny specks.

One of my favorite theologians, Dr. Richard Lennan, says that light is favored over darkness. "For darkness to win, it must win 100 percent. But for light to win, it only needs to win 1 percent." Those are good odds! Light can spread so quickly.

We are children of the light.

Where is there light in your life? Even on these dark, cold days in the northern hemisphere, the sun still rises. We might not have bright, warm sunlight, but during the daytime hours, even on cloudy days when we cannot see the sun, the sun is there. Jesus is here for us, calling our name, inviting us to follow him. Even if we cannot see him, we know he is there, whispering to us, "Come, live in the light. . . . We are called to act with justice, we are called to love tenderly, we are called to serve one another, to walk humbly with God!"

Fourth Sunday in Ordinary Time
God's mad miracle of making do

JANET SCHLICHTING, OP

Zephaniah 2:3; 3:12–13
Psalm 146:6–7, 8–9, 9–10
1 Corinthians 1:26–31
Matthew 5:1–12a

Today we hear of remnants: of foolishness, of God's wisdom and tenderness—and in our gospel, the beatitudes, that is, Jesus's understanding of God's agenda and who really are first in importance. Our readings from the prophet Zephaniah and the First Letter to the Corinthians already challenge our day-to-day assumptions, as they were meant to do in the times they were written. And then we have those remarkable beatitudes, part of what you might call Jesus's Inaugural Address as he initiates the New Covenant.

Consider the lowly. God's watch over the remnant, the ones who will prove to be the most faithful even though they are the lowest in social status and the most sinned against and the outsiders and leftovers. They are called the *anawim* of God, and Zephaniah declares that they will be the firm foundation of the New Israel.

The lowly. Being not so far from Christmas, we remember the hymns and carols we sang—and lots of them have the words "lowly" or "lowliness" in them. This is pure romance. Lowliness is not lovely or of itself doesn't confer holiness on anybody.

The Old Testament story of the Babylonian captivity tells us that when the enemy conquered the nation and destroyed Jerusalem and carried the population and all its treasures and possessions into slavery—the lowly ones, the poor of the land, were left to make do, to make what life they could in the rubble of towns and the decimated fields of grain. The lowly were not even good enough for slavery!

So, who are the lowly in our world? Well, you know where not to go in your city. You don't want to be in their neighborhood. In Jesus's time: lepers, tax collectors and sinners. In our time: high school dropouts dealing drugs as their only source of cash, the neglected elderly, the men who live under the bridges, the dumpster divers—and all over the world refugees from wars and terror that have sent them fleeing, homeless, unwelcomed, stopped at some border with nothing left but fading hope.

And then there are Paul's beloved but exasperating Corinthian Christians, who like to boast about their spiritual gifts; and groups of the converted who are tussling with each other about their standing. Paul reminds them that in the bustling city of Corinth, they are viewed as lowborn and uneducated—"foolish" is Paul's word—and that God's wisdom prefers it that way. So if you have any claim to swaggering around all puffed up, it's only God you have to thank.

And then come the beatitudes, consoling and hopeful. Some of Jesus's first words about the New Covenant. There are several lovely musical settings that are so poetic and uplifting and inspiring. But strip away the music; don't get all caught up again in romance. Without the harmonies and the upbeat lyrics, they're really pretty stark. Listen again. Consider again.

Now you're one of the poor as in Luke, or one of Matthew's poor in spirit—this is not an honor, or something to aspire to—it's more likely a result of your misfortune—because your spirit has shriveled as you've spent a life of worry and scraping to feed your family, and there is simply nothing left in you that offers the leisure to gather round the fire and sing, or the time and means to celebrate the feasts devotedly, or make plans to improve your lot.

I wonder how you'll take the news of your blessedness. Here's my guess. (Eyebrows up, mouth agape): Blessed? How dare you tell me my life is blessed!! That I'm one of God's favored? That I'm going to possess the kingdom of God? Tell me how, then, because I haven't seen any kingdom around here. It's all in the hands of the rich people, the landowners, and its gates are guarded by the know-it-all Pharisees who look down their noses at us. Kingdom? Blessed? Get over it. God hasn't been interested in us for a very long time.

And the mourners? You can talk about comfort.... Does anyone really stop mourning the loss of loved ones? How can you comfort a widow whose spouse's death has ripped out her heart? Who can comfort a mother who loses her babies, one after another? We have arms to embrace and food to bring over, small comforts. But you can't bring them back—and that's the comfort they want. So where's the blessing?

And the meek? Inherit the land? The powerless, the paupers like us? Our own rich people steal our tiny plots out from under us, and in comes Caesar and his bullying troops and there's nothing we can say or do that won't get us run through with a sword. Afraid you're starting a rebellion.

Justice? There is none—it is as the prophets always said. No justice, no peace, no return of stolen goods or lands, no payback for the swindled and the preyed-upon, like widows and orphans. No just judge that will hear us, no lawyer to take our side. Where are God's prophets now to preach about how God favors us and show us just how that plays out?

Suffering people of every place and time are not likely to call themselves blessed. They find no shred of grace in their poverty, their losses, and the ill-treatment they bear. They live in fear and on the edge of despair. Their labors are hard, their earnings never enough to cover their basic needs, to fill their hungry children, to pay the past-due rent and keep the lights on.

The point is, the beatitudes are really not about happy people. One must be very cautious of suggesting to the discouraged and hurting that they are oh so blessed because they're in this lousy state of affairs.

So—are the beatitudes about us?

Farther down the list, we can see work that we can aspire to—the mercy, the uprightness of heart, the peacemaking. And there is no doubt that we are inescapably called to be voices for the voiceless, and to suffer for it.

But what we can't allow ourselves to get stuck in, as before with "lowly"—either romanticizing the beatitudes, or spiritualizing them—is to work on them as virtues, or as states of soul to be practiced diligently so we become more Christ-like . . . let's see . . . how should I work on lowliness, how can I be more poor, or practice poverty of spirit, or be more meek and humble . . . and so on.

Instead, I think we have a different calling. Or drenching. It's baptism, and it immerses us in beatitude. To me, this means we are the ones seized by and sent by Christ Jesus and the Spirit as blessing—to be blessing and to give blessing to those who cannot see any blessing anywhere—and try to be a living word of God to them by witnessing as Christ bearers. Paul says "Other Christs."

There's a phrase used by the poor, and perhaps by some of our own ancestors in times gone by or in the Great Depression. When the resources are running out, when there is little left in the coffers or the cupboard, the woman will sigh, and then straighten up with resolve and say, "We'll make do. We'll just have to make do."

This is exactly what God is about. What God has been up to for all eternity. Our great Lover has, by the mystery of Incarnation and the victory over sin and death, erased the distance between us—that is between us and God, and also us and each other—and decided to get impossibly tangled up with humanity—and most mysterious of all, to include us in this immeasurable, magnificent outpouring of love. Sharing it. Giving it away.

This divine project of enlisting humans is more than chancy. It's divinely insane. We are absolutely not suitable for the honor or the labor. We're always falling on our faces. We're always making promises we don't keep. We can behave so badly. After all these years, we still haven't convinced the world of God's love and peace and justice. Why did God choose to make do with us? Had God run out of anything else?

Catherine of Siena asks God flat out: "O Mad Lover! And you have need of your creature? . . . You act as if you could not live without her, in spite of being the Source of Life itself. . . . Why then are you so mad? Because you have fallen in love with what you yourself have made! . . ." Catherine goes on to observe that God seems to be drunk with desire for her salvation: "You clothed yourself in our humanity, and nearer than that you could not have come." (A drunken God. Well, that might explain it.)

So today, we're offered this glimpse into the Mystery: God is "making do" by his covenant with humanity. It's his show. We certainly don't remember auditioning. We forget who we are. But God is remarkably persistent even though we, his human agents and carriers of the good news, are reluctant, and wish we had the chance to say "no" a bit more loudly. But God so loves the little ones, the poor ones, the sinned against and the sinners—and yes, us—who are some-where in there, but have this commission: Be who you are to show Christ to them.

There's nothing to do but stand in wonder at God's mad miracle of making do—and then get out there and bring blessing.

After evening prayer, we Dominicans sing a hymn to Saint Dominic. The last words we sing are these: "Preacher of grace, unite us with the blessed."

I used to think we were referring to the saints in heaven. Now? Not so much.

Fifth Sunday in Ordinary Time

Hunger and mercy in our time

KRISANNE VAILLANCOURT MURPHY

Isaiah 58:7–10
Psalm 112:4–5, 6–7, 8–9
1 Corinthians 2:1–5
Matthew 5:13–16

Two months ago I had the privilege of visiting our Lakota and Dakota brothers and sisters at Standing Rock Reservation in North Dakota. Reservations are among the hungriest places to live in the United States. Twenty-three percent of the Native Americans in the U.S. have terrible access to "adequate food"—almost twice the national average. A Lakota elder named Terrance told me of the 79 percent unemployment rate at Standing Rock.

Hunger can be hard to see. Even when it is noticed, it can be so easy to look away. Hunger isn't just on reservations. It exists in my neighborhood in the District of Columbia. Rural, urban, local or global—hunger doesn't discriminate. Today's reading from Isaiah talks about hunger and foreshadows Jesus's teaching on mercy. Isaiah predicts a chasm between what God intends for us and our tendency toward human sinfulness—notably this *absence* of mercy. Isaiah condemns false fasting . . . religious observances that show no mercy. Isaiah says we will know this "false fasting" because it results in exploitation and oppression . . . not reforms of the heart and actions that restore.

When I was in Kenya last month, a promising middle-income country in East Africa, the minister of health told us that one in four kids in the country is stunted—so chronically undernourished that the brain stops fully developing, dramatically weakening a child's ability to learn and thrive. As a mom of three, this literally took my breath away.

Images from Standing Rock and Kenya rushed to my mind when I read Isaiah. He says, "Share your bread with the hungry, shelter the oppressed and clothe the naked." These words ring familiar because seven hundred years after Isaiah, Jesus taught these same words. In the Church we refer to these as corporal works of mercy.

My visits to Standing Rock and Kenya occurred as Pope Francis's Jubilee Year of Mercy was coming to a close. The pope opened the Year of Mercy in Advent 2015 to promote a culture of mercy.

He calls mercy "the beating heart of the Gospel."

And so it is that the prophet Isaiah, Jesus, and Pope Francis each observe in their time a similar lack of mercy. And in response, they beckon God's people to be merciful. To live mercifully.

But what does living mercifully look like? How shall we cry out that the Lord responds: *Here I am!*? Mercy requires a change in heart and a transformation at our core. *Living mercifully* means giving from my whole heart so that my hands, my feet, my voice, my actions mimic God's reconciling and restorative work in the world.

Pope Francis says, "True mercy—*the mercy God gives to us and teaches us*—demands justice." He poses these questions:

- In your life, and in your faith community, how do you work for justice?

- Do you seek to address the root causes of problems that affect those who are vulnerable?
- Hungry people are often vulnerable and oppressed. So what does hunger look like in our time?

One in five Latino households struggles to put food on the table—almost double the rate for white households. And nearly half of all African American children younger than six live in poverty.

"Removing from our midst oppression," as Isaiah says, means we need to address the systems that make it hard for hungry people to feed themselves and flourish to their full potential.

Today in the United States, hunger has the face of a fifth grade child named Rosie in Collbran, Colorado, struggling to get through the morning's lesson on an empty stomach.

Around the globe today, nearly eight hundred million people will experience hunger.

Hunger has the face of a Syrian mother named Myriam who fled to Turkey along with her four children.

Hunger has the face of a South Sudanese teenage girl named Esther who fled violence in her village and now lives in a crowded refugee camp in Northern Kenya.

Sharing bread with the hungry is living mercifully. And our response to hunger must be the kind of mercy that demands justice and action.

In Matthew's gospel reading, Jesus offers some helpful guidance on how to live mercifully. He challenges us to be "light that breaks forth" and calls us to be "salt of the earth." That's a tall order!

What a humbling idea for Christ followers of any time!

In our time there are people named Rosie, Myriam, and Esther.

My brothers and sisters, we are characters in God's *amazing story of life*. To partake in God's work in the world, we must first see God's light in order to be God's light.

As believers we know God's light is among us. But so is oppression. Isaiah, Jesus, Pope Francis each say that to see God's light, we have to recognize oppression and sin. First we have to look inward...to discern oppression's many forms like unchecked materialism, privilege, and greed that lead to human and structural sin.

By beginning to remove the blinding, stifling oppression within us, we can more readily recognize oppression around us. We can see hunger and not look away. With God's grace we can stare down and confront the oppression that nearly blinds us to God's saving light.

God wants our fast to be mercy-led with transformed hearts. Then we can share God's mercy and be disciples of salt and light. Brothers and sisters, mercy opens our eyes to see God's light and opens our ears to hear God's unmistakable response: *Here I Am.*

Sixth Sunday in Ordinary Time
Fulfilling the law and the prophets

KATE OTT

Sirach 15:15–20
Psalm 119:1–2, 4–5, 17–18, 33–34
1 Corinthians 2:6–10
Matthew 5:17–37

Rules! I have been known to break them. In fact, becoming a Catholic feminist theologian feels like one long journey of breaking rules.

Perhaps that is why I have always struggled with today's gospel text in Matthew 5:17–37. s

After the description of Jesus's ministry starting in chapter four, Matthew's Gospel in chapter five depicts Jesus in front of a crowd with the disciples, laying out what probably appears to the crowd as "new teachings." The passages, including the beatitudes and the comparisons with salt and light, paint a picture of suffering and deferred reward. By the time we reach the law of the prophets, Jesus is keen to remind the crowd and disciples that these are not *new* teachings.

As Jesus says in verse 17, he did not "come to abolish the law or the prophets . . . but to fulfill." Our first reading from Sirach also reinforces the message that following the commandments is the path to God's favor. (Some interpretations of this gospel passage are anti-Jewish when read as Jesus being the fulfillment of the law and prophets and establishing a new law. Jesus does not say anything about establishing a new law.) Jesus proceeds to detail what he means regarding "fulfillment" by using a few commandments as examples.

Like Jesus, let's take some examples related to the commandments. I recently returned from El Salvador, celebrating the legacy of—now canonized—Saint Oscar Romero. In the face of state exploitation and brutality, he spoke up for the powerless when many other church leaders stayed silent or even supported the military. There were others at the time who sought to fight back lest they also be killed like Romero. Many of their friends and family members were murdered or disappeared. As citizens seeking to take back their lives, they took up arms in a civil war. They broke the commandment: Do not kill. Some ask, "Is self-defense killing? Or what does one do when there are no options left?" Do we make exceptions for this commandment and on what basis?

What about observing the Sabbath? For example, Jesus's healing of the blind man happens on the Sabbath and breaks purity laws. Jesus touches the blind man—someone deemed unclean, as blindness was a mark of being born carrying a sin of his parents. The healing might be construed as work on the Sabbath, which is forbidden by the codes as well. Afterward, the Pharisees are upset by Jesus's healing of the blind man. They question the man and proceed to throw him out of the temple. In response to the Pharisees, Jesus suggests that they are sinful for not "seeing" the real meaning of the law and need for healing (John 9:39–41). In this statement, similar to other passages in the gospels, Jesus suggests that those who enforce the purity codes for the sake of enforcement with no acknowledgment of the context are "blind" and not seeing clearly.

What about lying? The eighth commandment seems direct and unequivocal in its stance toward lying; the rest of the

Bible texts are not as clear cut. There are numerous passages that suggest that people should be honest in their speech (Matt 5:37) and put away falsehoods (Eph 4:25), and that God detests lying (Prov 12:22). Other passages show God telling prophets to lie in order to carry out their work (Exod 3:18, 1 Sam 16: 2). In still other cases, such as that of Rahab who hides the Israelites in Jericho (Josh 2:1–16), figures are rewarded after lying. Jesus himself is depicted as lying to the disciples about going to a feast (John 7:2–10). Might it be more accurate to say that lying is tolerated or understandable in service of a good intention? For example, Rahab's intention of saving the Israelites and her family is deemed faithful, even if she had to lie to do so. Here we might say, the intention is not to lie but to save the Israelites. Some ethicists call this the principle of double effect.

Jesus's interpretation is more comprehensive than a legalistic reading of commandments. This is what we might in ethics call focusing on the "spirit" of the law. In fact, Jesus is specifically calling the crowd to discern the meaning of the commandments for themselves. The religious authorities are not the final arbiters or even correct in their interpretation. Jesus remarks, "unless your righteousness surpasses that of the scribes and Pharisees, you will not enter the kingdom of heaven" (Matt 5:20). To Jesus's call for greater discernment and attention to the spirit of the law as I've called it, Paul reminds the community at Corinth in our second reading from 1 Corinthians 2 that we need to continually seek wisdom and listen for the Spirit, as God's work is not yet fulfilled.

This reminds me of Martin Luther King Jr.'s response in his famous "Letter from a Birmingham Jail" to those who criticized him for breaking laws during his nonviolent protests against white racism:

> One may well ask, "How can you advocate breaking some laws and obeying others?" The answer is found

in the fact that there are two types of laws: there are just laws, and there are unjust laws. I would agree with St. Augustine that "An unjust law is no law at all."

The racist laws and practices that King and those in the civil rights movement sought to overturn were unjust. Throughout history, those with power have established and enforced laws, rules, even claimed they were fulfilling the commandments at the expense of the powerless.

How do we follow Jesus in fulfilling the law and the prophets? For example, should a child who is experiencing sexual, emotional, or physical abuse by a parent stay silent so as not to dishonor their father or mother? Of course not! Speaking the truth about abuse in families, even church families, is necessary.

As the gospel reading ends with Jesus saying, "Let your 'Yes' mean 'Yes' and your 'No' mean 'No'" (Matt 5:37), we must remember: ethics—rules and commandments—are not lived in a philosophical abstraction. Jesus reminds us that following the law and the prophets is difficult work, in need of discernment, open to the Spirit, and guided by integrity. Even though we often fail to fulfill the law and prophets' intention, we must continue to strive toward that work with a spirit of love and welcome. As our gospel passage ends, Jesus continues by reminding the crowd and disciples to love their enemies and greet the stranger.

Seventh Sunday in Ordinary Time

A higher level of justice

EMILY CORTINA

Leviticus 19:1–2, 17–18
Psalm 103:1–2, 3–4, 8, 10, 12–13
1 Corinthians 3:16–23
Matthew 5:38–48

Who are your enemies?

Doris Hernandez lost her son Freddie seven years ago, when he was shot and killed on the streets of Chicago by an unknown assailant. By anyone's standards, her son's murderer is now her enemy, and it would be perfectly reasonable for her to wake up each morning filled with a burning desire for justice. And she does, but not the kind of justice one might imagine.

Twice a month, Doris sits with us in a circle at Kolbe House with families who have loved ones incarcerated. Mothers talk about their sons being accused of horrific crimes—even murder.

When Doris speaks, her message always centers on one thing: love. With her love for Freddie, she has opened her heart to all who are affected by violence, including those pulling the trigger. She has come to think of them—including her own son's murderer—as her own children. She is building a higher justice—one that seems more in line with God's plan for humanity.

It is this justice that Jesus illuminates in this week's gospel. He begins by calling out the old law of an eye for an eye, a tooth for a tooth. To modern ears the old law sounds like an extremely harsh system of punishment, but we misinterpret. It was actually a guide to make sure that punishments were proportionate to the wrong committed, not in excess. It was a reasonable way to administer consequences for laws broken.

But in this gospel passage, Jesus is calling us to go deeper than reason: turn the other cheek, walk two miles, give not just your outer garment but your inner garment as well. With these three examples, Jesus is not calling us to roll over and be used by our enemies. Rather, he is calling us to love. He is calling us to radical, creative, nonviolent love that strips the oppressor of control, restores the dignity of the one oppressed, and opens the door for a transformation of the relationship.

We are all called to apply this approach in our everyday lives, to love those who we consider to be our personal enemies. But we can also apply it to structures in our society, especially the structure of incarceration. In the United States, incarceration has become the go-to punishment used to keep those we have judged to be enemies out of our communities.

How can we apply Jesus's vision of justice to criminal justice and incarceration? Beyond addressing gross injustices in the current system, especially against people of color, responding to Jesus's call would completely transform the way justice is administered in our communities.

A growing consensus around the world—including within the Catholic Church and here at Kolbe House—is promoting a philosophy known as restorative justice. Restorative justice shifts the central focus of justice from punishment to healing. Healing means that the justice process cannot be dedicated to punishing those who have done wrong, but must be grounded in an understanding of the harm caused, so that consequences can be carefully agreed upon to address that harm.

Restorative justice also emphasizes the importance of the community, meaning we all have a role to play. Peace circles, restorative courts, building relationships with those affected by incarceration, including families and those who have completed their sentences—even changing the way we talk about people who have committed crimes as if they were villains—these are some places to start. These are tools that can involve the accused, victims, families, and community members in dialogues that lead to accountability, healing, and safer, healthier communities.

This approach to justice comes closer not only to what Jesus envisions, but also to the law given to Moses in the first reading, not to seek revenge but rather to love, to transform enemies into neighbors.

This justice practices the kindness and mercy of God expressed in the psalm.

This justice leans toward the godly "foolishness" that Saint Paul calls us to in the second reading. It is this foolishness that empowers a grieving mother to act out of love for her son's murderer, empowers us to go an extra mile and turn the other cheek.

Yes, Jesus is calling us to a higher level of justice—one that goes deeper than reason, one that lights our hearts on fire with a love that allows us to look at an enemy and see instead a brother or sister.

Eighth Sunday in Ordinary Time

Being held in God's maternal arms

RHONDA MISKA

Isaiah 49:14–15
Psalm 62:2–3, 6–7, 8–9
1 Corinthians 4:1–5
Matthew 6:24–34

Though a mother should forget her child, I will not forget you. What a powerful, intimate image Isaiah offers us in today's reading—the promise that God's love is more stead-fast and committed than that of a mother holding her infant. We have all seen a mother holding a sleeping baby—perhaps the most basic, elemental love there is. She is the source of nourishment, warmth, care, affection, everything that is needed. The mother gives of herself completely and the baby receives instinctively and completely this total gift. This tender mother-love is a powerful image for our bond with our loving and merciful Creator.

And yet, in the same passage from Isaiah, we hear the cry, "The Lord has forsaken me!" These anguished words res-onate when we experience the felt sense of abandonment and cry out to God in distress—such moments are part of our journey of faith. Scripture does not shy away from recogniz-ing that reality. There is space in the Bible for honest, anguished lament—here in Isaiah and in many other places. This is genuine prayer, and a sign of faith, not faithlessness. In our lives—as in this passage—trust and lament often exist side by side.

We may feel distant from God, but Isaiah encourages us by reminding us that the fierce, intimate Divine love is always there. While the feeling of abandonment is present and can even be acute, the fact is that we are never outside this circle of God's *agape*, never outside those loving, caring maternal arms.

We respond to Isaiah's promise with the psalmist's words, "Rest in God alone, my soul." The repetition: alone, only, alone. Nowhere else is unconditional love and mercy to be found. We respond to radical love with radical trust. We can crawl into God's lap in prayer and rest there completely.

The "trust and resting in God" that our psalm names take on a new dimension when read beside today's gospel which tells us to be like birds and flowers, free from worry about tomorrow. The Sermon on the Mount is filled with challenging teachings. Today's gospel offers plenty of challenge as well. Jesus points to the bountiful goodness of creation, the abundance found in the natural world. If other creatures do not worry, why should we? Of course, this is much easier said than done, which is perhaps why in the eucharistic liturgy we pray, "Protect us from all anxiety."

Perhaps you come to today's readings with a heart and mind filled with all kinds of concerns—family and friends who are struggling, health problems, financial worries, professional turmoil. Or maybe you, like me, are heartsick at the violence and injustice in our world and worried about what the future holds in increasingly uncertain times.

Those who heard these words preached by Jesus would have had hearts and minds filled with very real concerns too: they were Jews living under Roman occupation who faced the constant threat of violent repression. They were heavily taxed and longed for deliverance by a promised messiah. If you're from a class-comfortable background like me, try to imagine hearing these words if you really had to struggle to have adequate food, drink, and clothing. In the face of this, Jesus advised them to seek God's kingdom and righteousness. What transformation was Jesus offering the original listeners of his words? What transformation does Jesus offer us today?

The teaching to seek God's kingdom and not to worry is paired with the insightful observation that we must choose between serving God and serving mammon—which is wealth. If we are honest, can we observe in ourselves how our worries lead us to grasp, to cling, to develop what Saint Ignatius of Loyola termed disordered attachments. We seek security outside that only place where security can be found. And the more we cling, the smaller our world gets, the more our heart turns in on itself and away from God and our brothers and sisters.

Jesus's invitation is to "seek first God's kingdom." These words offer both great challenge and great freedom. Tremendous space is created when we can step away from our internal broken record of worries and concerns and the unhealthy behaviors we are drawn into when we seek security in anything but our loving, trustworthy God. In freedom from anxiety, there is freedom for becoming who we are truly meant to be—just as the birds and the lilies live out the fullness of who they are. We are free to live outside the dominant cultural ethos and within the light of beloved community. While our worries are legitimate, we are invited today to return over and over again with eternal trust to the loving arms of our God, just like the baby resting completely in the loving arms of a mother.

Twelfth Sunday in Ordinary Time

Let us shrill in the night*

LÉO LUSHOMBO

Jeremiah 20:10–13
Psalm 69:8–10, 14, 17, 33–35
Romans 5:12–15
Matthew 10:26–33

"Do not be afraid"! Jesus's call to not be afraid of those who kill the body but cannot kill the soul—rather, to be afraid of the one who can destroy both soul and body in Gehenna—speaks to all of us, men and women of the world.

Jesus's call speaks in a more particular way to all the women of the world subjected to atrocities of gender-based violence, rape, and killing. I am especially thinking of the women of my country, the Democratic Republic of the Congo. Since the Rwandan genocide in 1994, Congolese women have been exposed to widespread rape with extreme violence, particularly in the regions of our country rich in mineral wealth, more so than in agricultural areas. Unfortunately, the Congolese case is not unique: the evil of the rape

---

*To "shrill" is to cry out loudly and emotionally. Here, another translation of the original French is "dispel the darkness."

147

of women is increasing in war zones worldwide, even in the Global North countries and in times of peace.

Yet, Jesus keeps on calling to all of us, women and men: *"Fear no one.... Do not be afraid of those who kill the body but cannot kill the soul; rather, be afraid of the one who can destroy both soul and body in Gehenna."* Such a call resonates strongly for the people of the Democratic Republic of the Congo, particularly women, whose nearly five thousand bodies have been violated by conflicts since the Rwandan genocide, to rise and live and recover their strength in faith and hope. Indeed, in the eastern Democratic Republic of Congo, people are still going through profound suffering—a suffering that can be related to that of the people of Israel described in the first reading—and they are courageously acting to respond. Women and men keep giving their lives in service to others despite the danger of losing their own, like the woman who refused to obey the armed groups and killers who ordered her to separate Tutsi and Hutu during the genocide. She chose to risk her own life rather than expose the children to death.

Do not be afraid. Rise up, cry out in the night as did this Congolese mother and her husband, who, in the midst of the atrocity of the aftermath of the Rwandan genocide, went out answering the call for help from the United Nations High Commissioner for Refugees. They found a baby boy whose mother was dead in the road to Goma and saved him. This baby was still alive, suckling at his mother's breast. They took him, protected him, named him, and raised him as their own; the little boy survived and became a man. Yes, let us cry out in the night like the Congolese doctor Denis Mukwege. Not satisfied with earning money by treating women victims of atrocities of wars, he takes personal risks to denounce the evils that are destroying the lives of women and children.

Thus, do not be afraid, you people of Africa and elsewhere, whose hope is obstructed by the violence and selfishness of your presidents and governments who maintain themselves in power regardless of the constitutional presidential term limits. Do not be afraid, you whose lives in war zones are continually threatened, crushed, and sacrificed by warlords and political and economic interests. Jesus calls on you to not be afraid of those who kill your bodies, for they cannot kill your souls. "Are not two sparrows sold for a small coin? Yet not one of them falls to the ground without your Father's knowledge. Even all the hairs of your head are counted. So do not be afraid; you are worth more than many sparrows."

As the prophet Jeremiah guarantees us, the Lord hears the whisperings of his people. So, let's stand up and let no one take away the hope and power of faith that Jesus alone grants us. As the Lord exhorts his people in the Book of Lamentations, let us rise from the corner of every street and unite with those whose dignity as daughters and sons of God is totally denied, for they are all worth more than so many sparrows.

Thirteenth Sunday in Ordinary Time

Hospitality personified

CRISTA CARRICK MAHONEY

2 Kings 4:8–11, 14–16a
Psalm 89:2–3, 16–17, 18–19
Romans 6:3–4, 8–11
Matthew 10:37–42

On my daughter's third birthday a few years ago, we hosted a backyard barbecue to bring together our friends and family. As the rest of us rushed around getting everything ready, she sat on the front step of our house, watching and waiting for her guests to arrive. I had spent the week before in preparation—I was busy! But as I passed the front door on my way up the stairs that day, I stopped and looked at this little person, her knees tucked up, watching the driveway with great anticipation. When the first guest arrived, she ran across the front yard to greet them and walk them to the house. She did that again and again, for each guest, with a smile of joy and love on her face.

In today's readings, we are invited to consider hospitality in our relationships with others and with God. What does it take to receive others into our life? What does it take to receive God? What do we have to put aside? What are the fruits of hospitality? How is God reaching out to receive us?

150

In the first reading, the Shunammite woman welcomes Elisha, the holy man of God who has come to dine with her and her husband. Once they welcome him to their table, her hospitality goes a step further. She takes the initiative to create a space for him to stay. It is a unique moment in scripture as she—a married woman—puts forth this idea to her husband; but she is determined to receive him in her home and offer him a place to rest, to just *be*. Elisha, moved by her generosity toward him, asks God to reward her hospitality with a son, even though she and her husband are advanced in years. She opened her heart and home to the person in front of her, and she was rewarded for it with joy, love, and new life.

How often do we take the initiative, go the extra mile, reach out beyond our regular duties to offer hospitality? One of the most important parts of Saint Benedict's Rule encourages monks and nuns to "let all guests who arrive be received like Christ." It takes the monks out of their daily routine to encounter God in the other. In my ministry with college students, I see how getting caught up in the details can overrun the opportunity to receive others wholeheartedly, to love and be loved in the moment. It is easy to put other things first. It's satisfying to check off a list instead of looking at the person in front of you. So often we can get caught up in the demands of our daily lives. Life is fast-paced. I have emails to send, appointments and meetings and deadlines to make, bills to pay, responsibilities to attend to. It takes vulnerability to stop, to let God love me and receive me, to draw me into God's life so that I can then extend that love toward others. Yet that is what I long for, what we all long for—as Saint Augustine said, our hearts are restless until they rest in the Lord. We long to be welcomed as we are, to belong.

Jesus's words in today's gospel come at the end of instruction to the twelve apostles about what it means to be missionary disciples, to live in the "newness of life," as Paul puts it in his Letter to the Romans. It is not an easy path Jesus lays out for them. There are risks and challenges, hard choices to make about relationships and worldly possessions. One of these challenges is that we are called to receive those coming in the name of God, because hospitality is part of the call of Christian life. However, there are times when we don't want to stop and hear where God is calling us to be present, to welcome in love. We live in a period when our global world is growing smaller and smaller, but there is greater separation between us. Cell phones and social media can be great tools for connecting me to people far and wide, but do they also create a great divide between me and the person in front of me? My to-do list is important to keep life running smoothly, but if I miss a moment of connection because I'm too busy, can that list get in the way? Political tensions, racial tensions, religious tensions—there are plenty of areas that direct us to keep others at arm's length, to safely not engage. If I don't see eye-to-eye with someone, how can I welcome that person? Hospitality reminds us to live our Christian call to turn outward, to reach out, to love our neighbor, whoever that might be. It reminds us to encounter and receive Jesus in our lives through the other, known or unknown, alike or different, in a new way. As Sister Joan Chittister says, "Hospitality is the way we come out of ourselves. It is the first step toward dismantling the barriers of the world. Hospitality is the way we turn a prejudiced world around, one heart at a time."

Jesus is hospitality personified. How many times in the gospels do we read of Jesus inviting others to eat with him, of drawing people in from the margins to break bread and grow in relationship with him, to be loved? Jesus invites and receives us into life with him, and invites us to extend that hospitality and love to others.

When my little three-year-old daughter sat on that front step, I saw true hospitality. As I was busy with my to-do list and chores, my daughter sat with her open heart and hands, ready to receive. It is a model for me, not only of what it means to receive people in hospitality but also what I imagine God feels when receiving *us* with open hands and open heart: pure love and joy. And *that* can make us sing as the psalmist sings today, of the goodness of the Lord!

Fourteenth Sunday
in Ordinary Time

Sharing the burden

CHRISTINE ELISABETH BURKE, IBVM

Zechariah 9:9–10
Psalm 145:1–2, 8–9, 10–11, 13–14
Romans 8:9, 11–13
Matthew 11:25–30

Come to me all you who are heavy burdened . . .

It really helps when preparing a homily if the readings are relevant! And yes, today, many people are heavy burdened—by fear, financial insecurity, loneliness, and grief. While some societies creep back toward what once felt normal, others feel abandoned as the pandemic sweeps on. Here in the Philippines, as everywhere in the world, poor people carry the heaviest burdens. Isolation and physical distancing are impossible when a wall of cardboard or torn plastic separates a family of eight in one room from their neighbors. In every country people feel weighed down. Circumstances vary, *but our encounter with coronavirus and its unimaginable death toll has rammed home to us that we are interconnected, interdependent, and not controllers of the earth.*

And I wonder if you, like me, feel this pandemic is even more overwhelming because it is happening in our current

context? The ferocity of bushfires, droughts, floods, ty-
phoons, and melting ice-caps warn us that we face a challenge
that no vaccine can conquer. Frankly, climate change is deeply
scary. Young people urge us to rethink our way of living, to
recognize that we *belong* to Mother Earth and that she is not
ours to plunder. Theologians tell us that the extinction of a
species destroys another small revelation of God. This coronavirus "pause button" that shut down our world demands we
recognize our interconnectedness, rethink priorities, and
allow our hearts, minds, and actions to be changed.

I find it hard not to feel powerless and overwhelmed, and
it is from that place that I have meditated on these readings.
The prophet Zechariah, writing about five hundred years before Jesus, encouraged his people who felt overwhelmed with
the huge task of rebuilding the temple. He promised a new
style of leader, riding on a donkey (not an army tank!), using
his power in humility and simplicity to bring peace to the
whole earth. We might look around the world and say, "if
only we had that kind of leader today!" But we can all be leaders in small ways, choosing simplicity, working for peace. In
the second reading, Saint Paul assures us that we have the
Spirit of the risen Christ who helps us to choose well, to put
to death expectations and actions that are self-centered.

But it's our gospel text that speaks most strongly. "Come
to me you who are heavy burdened. . . ." This reading shows us
that Matthew's community was pondering the rich Wisdom
tradition in the Hebrew scriptures. These Wisdom books were
written in the last few centuries before the birth of Jesus. They
use female imagery to talk about God, and see her as guiding
them in their journey across the desert, welcoming people to
the banquet, meeting them in their daily lives, sitting with
them at the city gates, offering them hope, sharing their burdens. Wisdom (*Sophia* in Greek) is how they named God as
they encountered her in the struggles of everyday life. Her
message of hope calls human beings to a new way of living.

Like us, the early Christians had good reason to feel overwhelmed: they thought their dream ended when Jesus was brutally murdered by the religious and political authorities. But after their initial turmoil and bereavement, the women and men who followed him experienced that the God of love and compassion, the One at the heart of all Jesus's teaching, had worked something beyond anyone's imagining. Jesus's death was not the end. They came to realize that this man Jesus who was their friend, shared their burdens, celebrated many meals and feasts with them, and taught with such wisdom, was more than just a teacher; he was, in a very deep sense, *God* present with them. The Wisdom texts would have helped them make sense of such a possibility.

A few years after Jesus's death and resurrection, Saint Paul called Jesus the "Wisdom of God," and in these verses, Matthew's community placed Wisdom's words on Jesus's lips, so that Jesus claimed Wisdom's role as his own. God's Wisdom would be with them. They found their burden was shared and not heavy. Strengthened by the Spirit, they dared to go forward as a community, bound together by hope.

"Come to me . . . for I am meek and humble of heart. . . ." Meekness and humility do not get good press in the economic or political world. Yet humility is owning the truth about who we are: gifted yet weak, loved yet failing. With such honest self-knowledge, change is possible. As individuals, families, and societies, can we consider the small things each one of us can do, as well as the bigger things we must work for in collaboration with all people of good will? For example, some might find that two months of non-shopping enables them to contribute to groups advocating climate awareness. Others might help build peace through Caritas International or Doctors Without Borders or by helping out in their local Vincent de Paul center. Still others, like me, might find that one step is working to get a rat-proof compost system to help people who are poor reduce their rubbish! We can all take time to appreciate the beauty in nature and allow it to convert our hearts.

Today's readings challenge us. Can we have the humility to come as "little ones," asking Wisdom to help us to understand, to change, to live in a new way? Can we let go of some good things to allow a greater good to emerge? As with the early women and men who followed Jesus, Wisdom is offering to help carry our burden. Jesus's yoke is like an arm around our shoulders, a wonderful companion at our side, sharing the burden. Do we dare allow hope into our hearts, as Wisdom calls us to move beyond our confusion and grief, to listen and to change?

Fifteenth Sunday in Ordinary Time

We are the soil

Molleen Dupree-Dominguez

Isaiah 55:10–11
Psalm 65:10, 11, 12–13, 14
Romans 8:18–23
Matthew 13:1–23

The sower is out here sowing seeds. Tossing them willy-nilly onto all kinds of surfaces. What happens next?

Well, says Jesus, it all depends. . . . How's the soil?

Is there little of it, such that the seed is easily exposed and taken away by a strong breeze or a hungry bird?

Is the soil shallow, so that, because there's no room for the roots to descend, the seed might sprout immediately and perhaps grow for a short time but can't sustain that growth?

Or . . .

Is the soil black, rich, and humid? In other words, is it fertile? Is there enough space and time for the seed to extend its roots down into the darkness to suck up the smelly rot, transforming what was waste into something useful?

In my corner of the world—northern California of the United States—it feels like we're in a seed storm. The Sower is tossing out seeds from every angle, and into every heart, whether prepared soil, vacant lot or, more likely—some of both.

The seeds are flying on social media, with every hashtag and viral video. They're posted in signs on our front lawns; they're shouting into news cameras; they're marching in the streets; they're begging for oxygen to breathe. They are the seeds of racial justice.

These seeds demand that we acknowledge the fact that the United States as we know it was constructed on the land of the Indigenous and the backs of people of color—and that these communities have been blocked from participating in the harvest of this society. These seeds spotlight the role of Christianity in this reign of Whiteness, which has been constructed and rewarded as a way of life superior to all others. These seeds seek repair of the broken systems, institutions, and relationships left in the wake of White dominance.

These seeds land on the ground, scattered by a Sower not inclined to hold back, but also aware that only *some* will hear, understand, and bear fruit. Yes—it's a flurry of seeds, action, tweets, and marches now—but only some seeds will land on fertile ground—ground prepared to sustain healing for the long haul.

Now—imagine—you're the soil. You're the soil. I'm the soil.

Let us allow the Holy One to do what today's psalmist promises—break up our clods, shower the valleys, uproot that which chokes out life, and prepare the soil so that the seeds might yield a fruitful—and long-lasting—harvest.

To put it plainly, a year from now, after you've changed your social media profile picture back to your families and pets, after your book club has finished reading *White Fragility*, after you've marched until there are holes in your shoes, after you've called your state attorney general asking for changes in the way states investigate and prosecute police officers who kill citizens…will that seed still have nourishment to flourish?

Now I'm going to speak to my United States White sisters and brothers—because you folks of color certainly don't need another White lady telling you what to do.

White sisters and brothers, let us commit now to continuing to allow God to nourish that soil—nourish us—one year from now, five years from now, fifty years from now. Let's commit to listening to our sisters and brothers of color, to seeing with their eyes, and—most importantly—to stepping aside, trading our comfort for a cloak of justice, enacting meaningful and wide-reaching financial reparations to level the playing field, insisting we learn the unvarnished truth about the terrorism inflicted upon people of color by people who look like us. We've got to repent—as a people—for what we have done and build up our tolerance for the fight. We will get knocked down with grief, embarrassment, and shame at what has happened. And we must get back up—because if history has taught us anything, it is that the journey to racial healing will last for generations, with each lurch forward costing us untold numbers of Black lives.

The weeds and thorns of racial superiority have established excruciatingly deep roots in the institutions of the United States of America as well as in the hearts of Americans. As any skilled gardener will tell you, uprooting entrenched weeds takes persistence and focus.

God assures us through the words of Isaiah: My work is not wasted. I send out my word, says God, and it *will not* return to me until it has accomplished its work. God's word— these seeds thirsting for justice—will find fertile soil. God is our ultimate model of the skilled gardener—persistent and focused. Let her be our guide.

The psalmist imagines a fruitful harvest where the fields are lush with blossoms and the valleys blanketed with grain. The harvest is abundant and available to all.

We are not there yet. We may yet be far from this verdant vision.

But if we pause and pay attention, we can feel it coming. The stirring of the earth, the yearning of our hearts, brave roots reaching down into the dark muck, searching for nourishment there in the dark, moist, hidden nooks of earth. We witness the cautious breakthrough of a tendril, poking above the ground. Will it bear fruit that lasts? Depends on the soil.

Sixteenth Sunday in Ordinary Time

God is a good gardener

RUTH FEHLKER

Wisdom 12:13, 16–19
Psalm 86:5–6, 9–10, 15–16
Romans 8:26–27
Matthew 13:24–43

Just to be up front about it: I am a really bad gardener. Luckily I have only a balcony to keep track of, and even there plants tend to die before their time. Sometimes because I forget about them, sometimes because I think of them too often; always because I'm not patient enough to wait for them to grow, to figure out what they need in order to grow. I am always sorry when it happens (and miraculously there are some plants that survive my neglect), but so far that hasn't resulted in much improvement on my part—although there is a new attempt in the works just now.

Why do I tell you that? Because to me this gospel is all about growth in its different dimensions. And because I tend to be just as impatient with my own growth, and sometimes with that of others and the world in general. And I think I might not be the only one. Growth is something that to me seems only visible in hindsight. Growth consists mainly of hope, and thus is imbued with uncertainty.

In talking about the kingdom of heaven Jesus today gives us three parables—images that describe what the kingdom of heaven is like, or rather how it will come to be. And they all have to do with growth. That means the kingdom is not something that is suddenly there, fully formed and all-encompassing, but that it is emerging, still growing, slowly becoming.

The first parable, that of the grain and weeds, at first seems a little off-putting to me. It sounds like it is threatening judgment day. The image used is that of a man who sows good seed, and his enemy who sows weeds among them. And I immediately wonder: what am I? Good or bad? To be harvested or to be burned? But God knows we humans are almost never wholly one thing. We have within us both the potential to bear fruit and the potential to waste our energy and talents. And for most of us, both happen during our lifetimes. So maybe the parable is worth a closer look. The translation does not tell us this, but the weed the story refers to is called darnel. When young it is impossible to distinguish from wheat. And by the time you can tell them apart, their roots are entangled, so that pulling the weeds would mean losing the harvest. Thus the man decides to wait for the plants to fully grow and then take away the poisonous weed and burn it while the grain is harvested. That means this parable is a promise: God will wait for things to grow and bear fruit, in us and in the world. Judgment is wholly up to him, and he will never risk what is good and precious about us in order to throw out what is bad.

In the second parable, the image for the kingdom of heaven is the mustard seed, the tiny seed that grows into a large bush that draws birds to nest in it. I don't know if you have ever seen a black mustard seed. They are really tiny and it's easy to mistake one of them for a speck of dirt. That even a seed this small holds the potential for so much growth is simply amazing. And like this mustard seed, the kingdom of heaven starts out small, almost invisible. It is not something created by the great and powerful; it grows tall, and it draws people to it because they can feel God's love.

The third brief parable uses yeast as the image. I love this image, because I like baking bread. When I was little I used to do that with my dad. And I love how in a yeast dough the mushy mess becomes something else in my hands. Something solid, something that feels almost alive and that smells amazing. It only takes a tiny bit of yeast, some work and some time to transform the whole thing. In today's terms: if we manage to start somewhere, acting as if the kingdom of God is already here, the ripple effect will begin to change the world, will bring it together and create something wonderful and nourishing.

These are beautiful images. They speak of so much hope. They are there to encourage a community that feels small and helpless, like many early Christian communities did.

As Christians, it is our firm belief that all that is happening has a goal, a destination. We, and the world, are going somewhere, somewhere good. We live and work toward the kingdom of heaven. That's what we trust in when we follow Christ, when we follow the good news that God is love and the hope that love will win in the end, that the kingdom of heaven is growing in us and in our world.

To be perfectly honest, these days I find that hope sometimes hard to hold on to. There is so much bitter injustice among us that it's sometimes hard to breathe. There is so much suffering that the hope for justice, love, and healing we proclaim when we follow Christ sounds cynical and hollow, because we feel so helpless. It can be hard to trust in a good outcome.

As with gardening, I don't do too well with uncertainty. It's one of the reasons I sometimes hide my head in the sand, especially when it comes to questioning my own prejudice, checking my privilege, changing what feels familiar to me.

We all tend to find ways to mitigate and ignore the basic uncertainties of life that we are confronted with.

The coronavirus has shattered the feeling of security for many of us. Unrest about racial injustice, refugee camps at the borders of Europe, revelations of sexual abuse, especially within the Church, have done the same over the past months and years.

And although in its extent it might be a new experience for many of us, it is a very old and basic human experience, one that was certainly known to those who first heard these parables.

And even though I find it hard to come to terms with uncertainty, I also see those who help each other in the face of a devastating pandemic. I see those who protest against systems of racism and oppression, because they believe we can do better. I see people working against climate change who want to secure a hope for the future. I see survivors of abuse finding the courage to speak out, and others who support them. I see people looking for ways to help those trying to cross the Mediterranean Sea and those in refugee camps.

And so I cling to this unlikely hope: the hope that many small people in many small places who take many small steps will eventually change the face of the earth.

I might never be a good gardener, I might never be patient enough, or loving enough. I have no idea why some of my plants thrive, or if what I do as a pastoral worker will bear fruit. But luckily I don't have to know, because that is God's prerogative. God *is* a good gardener: He waits for us to grow, as persons, as a community, as a world. He waits for us to learn to trust that love will get us there.

Seventeenth Sunday in Ordinary Time

Drawing from the old and discovering the new

Maria Teresa Gastón

1 Kings 3:5, 7–12
Psalm 119:57, 72, 76–77, 127–128, 129–130
Romans 8:28–30
Matthew 13:44–52

It was two years ago this weekend that I found myself alone in our house of seventeen years having to prepare it for sale. John, my husband, had left already for a new start six states away. We had discerned this move together, leaning on our old Ignatian methods and even incorporating some new methods of problem clarification for creative decision-making I'd learned in my doctoral studies. The reasons for moving—closeness to family and new work—made sense, but my heart had not consented.

The stress of getting the un-updated 1953 house ready, including removal of broken basement tile and twelve years of Suzuki violin lesson notes, felt equivalent to the gut-wrenching experience of my comprehensive exams. The outpouring of loving help from friends who daily hauled away things to Goodwill or to the storage unit, others who cleaned the oven, painted, scraped tile, packed art, and took berries and perennials to replant in their yards filled me with overflowing gratitude and also made the goodbye all the more painful.

I tried to understand why it was so difficult to leave. As an immigrant from Cuba, I had not lived anywhere longer in my life. We raised the three boys in this community, and as a leader I had grown tremendously in my ministry with colleagues at Creighton. Just the previous January I had graduated with a PhD in organizational psychology. The years in Omaha were a treasure. The future was fuzzy.

When the pain of leaving was particularly acute, a wise friend urged me to be open to the new. That hit me, that simple word of advice. She made it sound so easy, "be open to the new." I felt the resistance in me like the clay dirt in this North Carolina soil that resists the seeds I want to plant in the garden in our rented house. Here, I experienced anxiety I had not known, and I lost weight. I was having trouble trusting that somehow all things would work together for the good. I tried to "offer it up," as my Mami had taught me to do with painful experiences. I prayed in solidarity with Syrian refugees and other displaced persons losing their homes under forced and violent conditions. I made a conscious choice to trust my life partner who was clearer about the rightness of this step and chose to join him daily in his discipline of twenty minutes of morning Centering Prayer.

Long ago I made a life choice for partnership with this man who loves God's commands. We entered freely into a covenant where we stated the intention to grow with each other "toward the fullness of love, freely witnessing to the presence of God in this world." We vowed to be "faithful in freeing each other to respond to the Spirit deep within, for our good and the good of the human family." Today's readings spoke to me about this marriage covenant and our ongoing practice of discernment in life, sitting down regularly alone, as a couple, and with the kids, to examine the good and the bad and to put the good in buckets, to learn from and treasure.

Biblical scholars are pretty sure the evangelist Matthew was referring to the Jewish scriptures and tradition as "the old" being brought out of the storehouse by the scribe discipled in the kingdom of heaven and Jesus's teaching about the reign of God as "the new." Some scholars think the old includes Jesus's teaching and the new is what came after Jesus's crucifixion for the Spirit-led community facing all of the challenges of being faithful and living the standards of the reign of God in the world.

Openness to the new in this transition of my life has come slowly for me this time, but it has slowly come. I have a very interesting job where I can draw from the "storehouse of the old and the new"—inside and around me. We are living near a dynamic and gifted young couple, our son and his wife, both in public justice ministries with two young children we are growing to know and adore (along with the chickens in the yard and the hipsters all around in Durham).

I appreciate in a new way the tension and dance of drawing from the old and discovering, creating, and pushing out the integrative new. We are in such a time. It feels urgent to draw from the deep wisdom of ancient practices of integrative wellness, community, healing, and justice-making, and to include the earth in our horizon of impact.

Do you understand all these things? Jesus asks us. How much I wish I could respond with a confident "yes" as Matthew tells us the disciples responded. It is such a confusing time.

Give your servants understanding hearts, O God. We know we are called according to your purpose and we are being conformed to the image of your Son. We have made life options to choose your reign above all else. Show us how to do this in partnership. Help us witness to your faithfulness in our covenants of love. We love your commands. Strengthen us in caring for each other and the earth.

Eighteenth Sunday
in Ordinary Time

The passion that moves the will to justice

CASEY STANTON

Isaiah 55:1–3
Psalm 145:8–9, 15–16, 17–18
Romans 8:35, 37–39
Matthew 14:13–21

Greetings—I'm coming to you from my home in Durham, North Carolina. In August. Where. It. Is. Hot! The heat dome that's sitting over most of the lower forty-eight is hovering over us and we're well into the days of summer when car seatbelts burn to the touch.

This heat matches the fire of my anger.

There is so much to be angry about these days.

Fr. Bryan Massingale, in an interview with *Commonweal*, reminds us, "What Saint Thomas of Aquinas says is beautiful: anger is the passion that moves the will to justice."

So maybe this anger doesn't have to just burn me up. Because there is so much I'm hot about.

I'm hot about the fact that Breonna Taylor's killers are still at large. And that between the time of this recording and your hearing it, the odds are disturbingly high that another Black life will be taken at the hands of law enforcement, with impunity.

I'm hot about some of our own U.S. bishops and their lawyers, bishops who are charged with being our shepherds. Are they protecting the flock? Feeding their hungry sheep? Or conspiring with the state for the legal right to slay their own?

I'm hot that women who are incarcerated in the state of North Carolina have been living on constant lockdown since March. This means confinement for twenty-three hours on their bed, with one hour a day to: make a phone call, visit with a chaplain or a social worker, take a shower, go to the canteen to buy a snack, head to the dayroom for a brief break, get fresh air. One hour a day. Staff at the facility are having to bring their own hand sanitizer and cleaning supplies, and the women's masks are fit for men's-sized faces.

I'm hot about the incessant polarization of a pandemic that leaves each of us faced with impossible decisions each day. Each of us individually having to navigate risk, costs, our health and safety, the health of others—weighing our sanity, our jobs, the well-being of our children.

No wonder my blood boils over into tears.

So when I go to meet Jesus today—when I ask him what he has for me, for you, for us—

I see a Jesus who also is hot with anger.

"*When Jesus heard of the death of John the Baptist, he withdrew in a boat to a deserted place by himself.*"

Jesus hears the news of his beloved cousin, the one who prepared a way in the desert, the one who proclaimed that a new kingdom was at hand, the one who predicted the Holy Spirit and fire of Jesus's ministry.

The one who also sat in prison, who sent his disciples to ask Jesus: *Are you the one who is to come?*

The one to whom Jesus responded by sending a message saying, "Tell him, tell him the lame walk, the blind are made to see, the deaf can hear, and the poor have good news proclaimed to them."

John the Baptist: the one who could see Jesus's call more clearly than most and who paid the ultimate price for his peculiar prophetic ministry.

"*When Jesus heard of the death of John the Baptist, he withdrew in a boat to a deserted place by himself*" (Matt 14:13).

Friends, as Jesus withdrew, I imagine him praying with anger and deep grief. Crying out to God his father: LORD, why do your rulers lack wisdom and live by fear, seeing the kingdom we've brought only through power-hungry eyes, wedded to violence and force, against this word of love and peace that we seek to proclaim?

What if today some of the good news for us is that Jesus shares with us—might even have put in us—our anger and our grief, so that we feel what he feels when he looks out and sees the world as it is today. Because if Jesus is with us in our anger, if we worship a Jesus who grieves, he can show us what to do with that anger and that grief.

Anger and grief can render me numb and hard, cold and mean, can turn me inward, onto myself and make me resentful of others. When people come asking me for things, I can often respond with resentment, annoyance, frustration, exhaustion.

But Jesus shows us another path in today's gospel. Jesus tells us it's okay to need to withdraw to the boat and rage, cry our hot tears—but then—see what he does—he turns back. He tells us: Remember how much you love this world. Look at the people you love, the people who draw near to you.

He turns and he sees the crowds that have gathered. He sees and is moved with great compassion.

Jesus withdraws but does not leave us alone; he turns back. He shows us the way to turn back, to not ever be cut off. He shows us what to do with our anger at John's beheading.

Jesus wants us to know that what Saint Paul tells us is truth: Nothing can cut us off, nothing can separate us from the love he has for us—not the White powers and principalities, not the homophobic legal briefings, not the misogyny that denies women's ability to image Christ, not state-sanctioned killings and federal executions.

Jesus returns and tells us to grieve, but then to return, to cure, to share what we have.

He tells us to trust that it will be enough when we bless it and offer it to God to give the increase.

These few loaves and couple of fish. This Bible and wonky wi-fi connection. Our baptism and the Word of God. What else do we think we need to do Jesus's love-work of curing sickness? Of feeding the thousands?

We're invited today with all our grief, whatever it is we carry, to sing out Isaiah's song of radical invitation to all who thirst and all who hunger.

> Come without paying and without cost
> Come—Catholic women, anguishing in your calling
>   and longing to find full recognition in your
>   church.
> Come—queer Catholics persecuted, discriminated
>   against, living in fear.
> Come—Black Americans, Black Catholics, constantly
>   in peril from the sword of White supremacy.
> Come—those who are suicidal, filled with anxiety,
>   suffering from depression and battling addiction.
> Come—all who are sick.
> Come if you are lonely and tired and weighed down
>   with grief.
> He beckons us:
> Come and sit on the grass. Rest here.
> You will eat well with me. Listen that you may have
>   life.
> I will renew you with the everlasting covenant.

Come, turn that hot anger into fuel that sustains
    your love of creation and the people of God en-
    trusted to your care.

Come and be changed, be renewed, be fed—by the
    same one who promises that no creature will be
    able to separate us from the love of God in
    Christ Jesus, but that in him we conquer over-
    whelmingly.

Amen.

Nineteenth Sunday
in Ordinary Time

Be not afraid

LOUISE AKERS, SC

1 Kings 19:9a, 11–13a
Psalm 85:9, 10, 11–12, 13–14
Romans 9:1–5
Matthew 14:22–33

Today's gospel is a familiar one: Jesus telling the apostles to get into a boat and cross the lake while he remains to take some time for prayer. A storm arises, the boat is floundering, and the apostles grow fearful and shout to Jesus for help. As he approaches them, seeming to walk on water, Jesus calls out to them, "Don't be afraid. It's me!" Peter tests Jesus, "If it's you, bid me come to you." Jesus does so but Peter, again, is filled with fear and calls out for help. Jesus immediately holds out his hand to comfort Peter, yet, at the same time, he reprimands him for his lack of faith. Thus, another story of the valiant Peter!

What causes fear in us? How do we handle it? In today's gospel, we hear clearly the encouraging words of Jesus: Don't be afraid. It's me! Remembering John Talbot's song we also hear the familiar comforting words: "Be not afraid, I go before you always. Come, follow me and I will give you rest."

In U.S. history, Franklin Delano Roosevelt's words have echoed long after he reassured the country: "The only thing we have to fear is fear itself." Why? Because fear paralyzes us. We don't have control. We feel helpless. On the other hand, hope activates us. Peace liberates us.

Once Peter and Jesus climbed into the boat, the wind died down. In the midst of the fierce storm, with Jesus, the disciples, calmer now, recognized his authority and knew they were safe. The gospels are full of moments like this. In the midst of fear and doubt, recognition of a loving presence results in not only outer but also inner peace. God is with us; God is within us. This is true when circumstances change, and at times we wonder if we can ever overcome the unexpected challenges in our lives. Whether it's losing a job, worrying about health care, getting a serious illness, the sudden death of a loved one, going off to college, relocating to another city or country, losing a good friend, worrying about drug addiction of a family member—add your concerns to this list.

We know our lives also exist within a broader context— that of our country and of the world!

Today this context is filled with new challenges, different fears: a possible nuclear war, terrorism on a global scale, climate change, a president who is unpredictable in both his words and his actions, the rise and expansion of theocratic beliefs threatening our democracy, increased poverty and homelessness overshadowed by an unprecedented refugee crisis, casualties of wars in Afghanistan, Iraq, Syria, and Congo. Again, the list goes on...

Some of you might remember the poem, "Desiderata." At one point we read: "Be at peace with God, whatever you conceive him to be. In the noisy confusion of life keep peace within your soul."

When we are at peace, hope emerges; when we are hopeful, we become agents of change. Agents of change believe in and work for a better tomorrow. Our God is a God of yesterday and today. Our God is also a God of tomorrow, of the future. "Be not afraid. I go before you. Be still and know that I am God."

Twentieth Sunday in Ordinary Time

A dialogue with Jesus

GERARDETTE PHILIPS, RSCJ

Isaiah 56:1, 6–7
Psalm 67:2–3, 5, 6, 8
Romans 11:13–15, 29–32
Matthew 15:21–28

We are well into the ordinary time of the year; but the readings of today are extraordinary because the Church calls us to respond to a dual yet single movement, which is to go within and experience God's unconditional mercy, and with that energy and passion to go beyond borders to share that mercy with all humanity—something that our world is in great need of now in this time of uncertainty.

Reflecting on the readings of today, I am reminded of an incident that took place a while ago. I took a few Christian friends of mine to a class in which Muslim, Buddhist, and Hindu students shared the way they pray and where God is in their lives. Their sharing was simple, deep, connected to significant moments in their lives. They ended their sharing by inviting all to pray together. A Muslim woman in the audience sitting next to my friend nudged her and pointing to her heart said—my God is here.

We shall find that we can enter into the value of others, be at home in their houses, and make the words of the prophet Isaiah a reality only by a genuine appreciation of their prayer of the heart. Whatever understanding of God that the heart holds, "*I will bring foreigners to my holy mountain. I will make them joyful in my house of prayer, says the Lord, 'for my house will be called a house of prayer for all the peoples.'*" Please note— for all the peoples; no one is excluded.

This takes me to a time when we were preparing special needs children for the Special Olympics. The race began and they noticed that one of their friends had fallen; they stopped in their tracks, went back, picked her up, and then all held hands as they ran to the finish line. This is the spirit that God is nurturing in us in the first reading, the spirit of excluding no one. This can happen by praying together, having compassion together.

The Breath of the Compassionate God breathes on all alike, extending the invitation and making God's mercy available for all. However we can feel this breath only if we are close enough. The Jews are the beloved of God and the Gentiles are favored and considered worthy of the good news even though they are referred to as pagans. Paul in the second reading is proud to be sent as their apostle. Israel, the chosen one, rejects God and Paul says, "*God never takes back his gifts or revokes his choice.*"

In today's gospel, Jesus is in a place that he has spoken of earlier. In Matthew 11:20–22:

> Then Jesus began to denounce the towns in which most of his miracles had been performed, because they did not repent. "Woe to you, Chorazin! Woe to you, Bethsaida! For if the miracles that were performed in you had been performed in Tyre and Sidon, they would have repented long ago in sack-

cloth and ashes. But I tell you, it will be more bearable for Tyre and Sidon on the day of judgment than for you.

In three verses Jesus mentions Tyre and Sidon twice.

A little earlier, Jesus is challenging the Pharisees and explaining to his disciples that it is not what goes into the mouth that makes us unclean but what comes out of the mouth, because what comes out of the mouth is from our heart.

After all this, now, Jesus has actually come to Tyre and Sidon with his disciples to give them a firsthand experience of what he has been telling them all along. Jesus knows that he is in Gentile territory. Jesus is met by a woman (which is usually the case). She comes to Jesus agitated, worried, and afraid about her daughter being possessed by a demon. When she is crying out I am sure the onlookers are waiting to see how this "good Jew" is going to respond. Jesus, a real actor, does not answer, not even a word. So, as the disciples have done elsewhere, they ask Jesus to send her away. Jesus now sides with his disciples and says to her, "*I was sent only to the lost sheep of the nation of Israel.*" It may be that the woman, a Canaanite, considering herself the lost sheep, feels Jesus has come for her. Her heart perhaps jumps for joy, since she is entitled to make her request. Now she does not shout but says only three words "*Lord, help me*" (what came out from her mouth was from the purity of her heart). Continuing to side with his disciples, Jesus says, "*It is not right to take the bread from the children and throw it to the dogs.*" The woman is neither offended nor does she take this as the last word. She replies with the same respect as before, "*Yes it is, Lord,*" she says. "*Even the dogs eat the crumbs that fall from their master's table.*" Jesus is both dumbfounded and proud of this woman!

A dialogue such as this can only happen in an atmosphere of honesty, humility, and acceptance. The woman feels this from Jesus and in the dialogue both are honest, Jesus as well as the woman. The woman can have this dialogue with Jesus because of the space provided by Jesus for her to be herself, to ask for what is uppermost in her heart, to claim her rights, to express her opinions, to experience her strength, and to know that someone does care. Jesus surprises us. He does not want the woman to have his faith for her request to be granted but commends her for the faith that she already has. Jesus's reply to her is: "*Woman, you have great faith! Your request is granted.*" It is a faith that defines mothers, a faith that I see in my own mother. The parallel of this event in the Gospel of Mark says, "*and when the woman went home, she found her child lying in the bed, and the demon gone*" (Mark 7:30). For sure, this woman is now happy and in peace.

In the beginning of the story, the woman comes crying out for pity and goes away perhaps smiling as her faith is affirmed and her request granted. Today, let us go to God, to Jesus, just the way we are. As he was in Tyre and Sidon, he is in our territory, waiting for us to approach him to ask, to cry out for his mercy for ourselves and for each other. And, like he said to the woman, he will say to us, "You have great faith, your request is granted." In today's readings we are invited to be in the house of prayer together, to exclude no one, to experience the mercy of God, and receive the promise that our requests will be granted in God's way and in God's time.

This invitation and promise, this acceptance and love received from Jesus will then give us the courage to go out with passion to proclaim the tender mercy of God to all as we sing with one voice the words of today's psalm, "*Let all the peoples praise you O Lord, let all the peoples praise you.*"

Twenty-first Sunday in Ordinary Time

The true way of authority

Catherine M. Mooney

Isaiah 22:19–23
Psalm 138:1–2, 2–3, 6, 8
Romans 11:33–36
Matthew 16:13–20

Authority figures command a lot of our attention. TV, radio, social media, and many of our own conversations revolve around politicians, business leaders, and even church leaders. Closer to home are the authority figures in our immediate lives: in our communities, workplaces, and homes. And most of us exercise authority of some sort as parents, teachers, supervisors, trusted friends, and so forth.

It's worth pondering how we think about and exercise authority. Are you eager to have more authority? If so, what do you hope to get out of having it? Admiration? Power to accomplish something? What is *true* authority? The two outsized authority figures in today's gospel, Jesus and Simon Peter, reveal something profound about the exercise of true authority—including our own.

At first glance, it seems that the authority of both Jesus and Simon are on the upswing. And that is what the world usually admires. Get more power; command more attention. Jesus *seems* to be garnering more power in this gospel. He asks his disciples: Who do people say is "the Son of Man"? The disciples offer up the names of several prophets, such as John the Baptist and Jeremiah.

Jesus then pivots and asks them, "But who do *you* say that I am?" Notably, Simon speaks up before the other disciples. He says to Jesus, you are the "Son of the living God," a title that seems to go further than "Son of Man" because it underlines the intrinsic connection between Jesus and the living God. And Simon also calls Jesus "the Christ," that is, the Messiah. Now, the Messiah is more than one of the great prophets; indeed, he is the one about whom the prophets prophesied. By calling Jesus the Messiah and the son of the living God, Simon acknowledges that Jesus has authority over all the prophets and, indeed, all humankind.

In return for having correctly identified the authority of Jesus, Simon seems to get a *quid pro quo*. And isn't that how authority often works in our world? You do something for someone powerful above you, and they in turn give you a leg up on the ladder of success. Jesus gives Simon two things. First, he gives him a new name—Peter—which means Rock. It's worth noting that Rock, unlike the nickname Rocky today, was not a personal name at this time in history; it simply meant "rock." Why would Jesus think this was a good new name for Simon? Well, it recalls a parable earlier in the gospel that contrasts the foolish person who builds a house on sand, which storms can destroy, with the wise person who builds a house on rock, which is thus able to withstand calamities. For Jesus, Peter is the Rock on which Jesus will build the Church, a church against which, Jesus says, even "the gates of the netherworld shall not prevail." The second thing that Jesus gives Peter is the keys to the very kingdom of heaven. What Peter binds on earth will be bound in heaven; what he looses on earth will be loosed in heaven.

Peter and Jesus both appear to be *uber* authority figures with tremendous power over other people. If we probe their authority further, however, it upends many of our conventional notions. In the very next passage of the gospel—after this one in today's reading—Jesus announces that he will suffer and be put to death. In the world's eyes, this positions Jesus with the weak—the "losers" some might say—and Peter, astonished to hear this, tells Jesus that this can't be. But Jesus rebukes him.

We have to recall that Peter repeatedly throughout his relationship with Jesus often didn't get what Jesus meant; he didn't understand Jesus's mission. Jesus was teaching Peter that the true way of authority is not exercising power over others but giving of oneself so that others may flourish. Again: The true way of authority is not exercising power over others, but giving of oneself so that others may flourish. At the Last Supper, when Jesus tried to wash Peter's feet, Peter protested. Jesus was showing Peter—to whom he'd given so much authority—that lording power over others, like the earthly kings and religious leaders whom Jesus critiqued, was not true leadership. Service and self-giving love were. Jesus drives home lessons that confound conventional logic, such as: "Whoever wants to become great among you must be your servant."

Jesus doesn't suffer and die because suffering and death are good in and of themselves, a false thread that has sometimes marred the tapestry of Christian history. No, he suffers and dies because he wants *all* to have life. Out of a sense of justice, he stands up to the powers-that-be that lord themselves over the powerless, and they turn on him and kill him. The kingdom whose keys he grants to Peter will not be a kingdom of alpha authoritarians having their way with everyone under them. Jesus is grooming Peter and the rest of the disciples for a new kind of kingdom, a kingdom of doing justice out of love for others.

Today's gospel still speaks today. So consider again the authority figures who populate the world and national stages—civic, church, and media personalities—and consider those you meet in your community and workplace. Most important, consider your own attitude toward gaining and exercising authority. How, like Jesus, can we—even at great risk to ourselves—stand up to today's kings and Pharisees ready to oppress others? And how, like Jesus, can we let love and life-giving service be the hallmarks of our own exercise of authority?

Twenty-second Sunday in Ordinary Time
Know better, do better

Nicole Trahan, FMI

Jeremiah 20:7–9
Psalm 63:2, 3–4, 5–6, 8–9
Romans 12:1–2
Matthew 16:21–27

I'm fairly active on social media. One of my favorite hashtags recently has been "know better, do better."

Something I've learned in recent months is how much I just don't know—about U.S. history... about African American history... about Church history... about how we came to be where we are right now as a nation. How did we come to be in the age we are today? It is extremely important to consider. If we don't know the answer, we cannot move forward.

Saint Paul exhorts us not to be conformed to this age. Wise words for us today. For what do we see in this age? We are in the midst of a global pandemic—hundreds of thousands have died preventable deaths, public health has become politicized, we see an uncovering of White nationalism—notice, not necessarily a rise, but an uncovering and perhaps a mainstreaming; systemic racism is still with us and the environment is in need of healing. This is the age in which we find ourselves. This is the age to which we cannot be conformed. We have to allow for a renewal of our minds... learning, growing, unlearning, challenging assumptions, revealing hidden biases....

Learning is important. But it can't stop there. Know better. Do better.

Once we know, we have an obligation. Once our eyes are opened to the reality around us, we cannot then close them and not see. Once we've heard the cry of the poor, the marginalized and the oppressed, we cannot unhear their voices or stop listening.

Not many of us like to rock the boat. We're often unsure, afraid of saying or doing the wrong thing. When faced with the same doubts, Saint Julie Billiart encouraged her sisters— "Better mistakes than paralysis." This is good advice. We can see that paralysis is not a valid option at this point. We must act—but never without prayer and discernment. Not only will this enable us to know what to do, it will give us the strength to continue when we are faced with obstacles, ridicule, and pushback.

For those will come. There will be struggle.

In an 1857 speech marking the twenty-third anniversary of the emancipation of the West Indies, Frederick Douglass asserted:

> The whole history of the progress of human liberty shows that all concessions yet made to her august claims have been born of earnest struggle.... If there is no struggle there is no progress. Those who profess to favor freedom and yet deprecate agitation are [men] who want crops without plowing up the ground; they want rain without thunder and lightning. They want the ocean without the awful roar of its many waters.

Progress cannot be realized without struggle. The Peters in our lives may say, "Heaven forbid!" And to that we should say, "Get behind me Satan. You are an obstacle to me." Sometimes we even have to say that to ourselves—"Get behind me Satan. You are an obstacle to me."

At times, in the midst of difficulty and struggle, we might say to ourselves, "Maybe I need to stop doing this. I'm tired. Tired of the ridicule. Tired of having to explain why I'm doing this. Just tired of the struggle." But if it is the Spirit of God— the spirit of justice and peace and mercy—that is acting within us, it will weigh on us and become like a fire burning within.

In her book *Redeeming Conflict*, Ann Garrido wrote:

When something matters to you, when something is important to you, it will damage both the relationship and your own sense of personal integrity not to at least bring it up. That impulse in our gut that propels us to speak...is an important voice to listen to. It needs to be guided by prudence, but also nurtured with compassion. It is a seed that the Holy Spirit has planted. It deserves water. It requires discernment. And it *will* come to fruition in time.

As in the case of our friend Jeremiah. Poor Jeremiah, reluctant prophet, didn't seem to know what he was getting himself into. Perhaps his youth kept him from foreseeing that his challenging words would bring him derision. He didn't seem to understand that people wouldn't be open to his words—his invitation to repentance, change, growth. He wanted to quit. To stop speaking these words that caused so much trouble for him. But he couldn't. And like Jeremiah, neither can we.

Because it's not about us. Our gospel today tells us that to be disciples we must deny ourselves, pick up our cross, and follow Jesus. To deny ourselves means we must stop making ourselves the center of our lives and put Jesus and his mission in this world at the center.

Jesus came in order to set the oppressed free, to proclaim liberty to captives, to offer sight to the blind, to proclaim a year acceptable to the Lord. This. This is our call. But we can't expect the path to be easy. It wasn't easy for Jeremiah, for Isaiah, for Amos, or for the apostles, the martyrs, the saints, Martin Luther King Jr., Medgar Evers, Rev. James Reeb, Claudette Colvin, and countless others.

"Do not conform yourself to this age, but be transformed by the renewal of your minds that you might know what is the will of God, what is good and pleasing and perfect."

Let us challenge ourselves to keep learning and growing, allowing God to transform us by the renewal of our minds, so we might act with courage in spite of the obstacles and struggles to bring about a time acceptable to the Lord.

Twenty-third Sunday in Ordinary Time

A people of reconciliation and restoration

KAREN CLIFTON

Ezekiel 33:7–9
Psalm 95:1–2, 6–7, 8–9
Romans 13:8–10
Matthew 18:15–20

Martin Luther King once stated in a sermon that we "must see that force begets force, hate begets hate, toughness begets toughness. And it is all a descending spiral, ultimately ending in destruction for all and everybody. Somebody must have sense enough and morality enough to cut off the chain of hate and the chain of evil in the universe. And you do that by love."

This is the message of today's readings. A call to love, compassion, reconciliation, and restoration.

What does it *really* mean to be a people of reconciliation and restoration?

The Church teaches that incidents of grave harm should be retributive, that they should have consequences for the offender. Remember Jesus's teachings about the sheep and goats. Christianity is not a feel-good religion.

But the Church also teaches that the response to harm must be restorative. This means we must seek to repair relationships and address the broader impacts of wrongdoing. We must recognize that we are responsible for one another's well-being and salvation. As we hear the religious leaders ask in Mark's Gospel, "Why does he eat with the tax collectors and sinners?" Jesus responds, "I did not come to call the righteous but sinners."

In Matthew's Gospel today, Jesus gives specific instructions about resolving conflicts. First, you sit down and talk about the conflict. And if there is no listening, you bring in someone else to sit down with you. This is very much in the spirit of restorative practices. Restorative practices mean listening to one another, coming to understand the hurt created by our actions and the actions of others and, where possible, seeking repair. Restorative practices mean that rather than responding out of anger or vengeance, we seek to truly understand the circumstances and the impact of wrongdoing on our individual relationships and the relationships around us. And with understanding comes the opportunity for transformation —repentance by those who caused harm and healing for those harmed.

These practices are countercultural. We live in a retributive society that says, "Someone has to pay and when they do, we walk away." But walking away or avoiding a conflict (though it surely is a lot easier!) is not restorative.

Making decisions in an arbitrary way (a way that creates winners or losers) rather than by consensus is not restorative. We all need to use restorative practices in our daily lives—with our families, in our workplaces, and especially in our churches. There are powerful examples of this. Those who have walked the path toward forgiveness despite having experienced some of the greatest hurt imaginable are evidence of the way mercy can heal our hearts and minds and strengthen our faith.

I have the privilege of working with the family members of murder victims. They cannot forget their deep wounds, but they don't attempt to ease their pain with vengeance. The families of murder victims who work to end the use of the death penalty in this country talk about their great loss. They also tell you that they do not want to inflict the same kind of loss on another family—the perpetrator's family. Vengeance does not bring back their loved one.

The families I work with say that forgiveness was not their immediate response. Understandably, it was anger and hate. But with time, through prayer and God's transformational grace and love, they manage to come to a place of forgiveness— or at least a place where, while demanding retribution, they do not demand vengeance. *They come to a place of peace* and are able to live for the good. They are not destroyed by hate. Instead, in that place of peace, they are restored.

I have also heard people who have committed great harm, after listening to how acts of violence like their own have affected families and communities, begin to understand for the first time the magnitude and scope of their offense. After learning that the families of their victims do not want vengeance, many work to give back, and in time, to forgive themselves. They too are restored.

The Eucharist is a reminder of how forgiveness is the *foundation* of our faith. Kathleen Hughes says it well:

> Each time the community assembles for the celebration of the Eucharist, it celebrates its own conversion journey as well, and it acknowledges the paradox of the Christian life: that we are saved sinners, liberated yet ever in need of deeper conversion...that God never ceases to call us to a new and more abundant life, that as sinners we are invited to trust in God's mercy.

We are all guests at the table. The Eucharist invites us to recognize not only our own sinfulness and seek forgiveness but also our responsibility to do the same for our brothers and sisters who are also at the table.

"For where two or three are gathered together in my name, there am I in the midst of them" (Matt 19–20).

May God be praised.

Twenty-fourth Sunday in Ordinary Time

The "good news" of forgiveness

JACQUELINE REGAN

Sirach 27:30—28:7
Psalm 103:1–2, 3–4, 9–10, 11–12
Romans 14:7–9
Matthew 18:21–35

In the early weeks of the global pandemic, I seemed to get daily emails from family and friends that included a favorite YouTube video recommendation. One in particular that caught my attention was hosted and produced by sitcom star John Krasinski, and entitled *Some Good News*. With his inimitable wit and warmth, Krasinski's quarantine web-series brought ordinary folks together in the same Zoom room with high powered celebrities like Boston's own Big Papi. They highlighted the goodness of humanity by celebrating people like high school prom-goers, 2020 graduates, dedicated and compassionate healthcare workers. Much to the disappointment of his 2.5 million subscribers, Krasinski sold his series to CBS after eight episodes. Production was hard to sustain, he said, and sadly, in mid-May, Krasinski's good news came to an end.

I'm tempted to return to the feel-good stories of *Some Good News* rather than sit with the discomfort and challenge of today's good news in the Gospel of Matthew. Peter's question, "Lord, if my sibling sins against me, how often must I forgive them? As many as seven times?" echoes through time and space, addressing me now in 2020. How hard it is to forgive injustices in church and society, to find a way through the anger I hold tight, never mind forgive countless times as Jesus instructs Peter. And in the face of great suffering and betrayal, it seems justifiable, sensible even, to withhold forgiveness—to blame, retaliate, seek retribution—even after the person who has done harm acknowledges their wrongdoing and commits to change. Yet the subtle pairing of the great commandment in today's gospel acclamation with Jesus's parable of the unforgiving servant comes to us as a double imperative: "love one another *and forgive* one another as I have loved and forgiven you." This is *the* good news of our faith, symbolized by the cross of Christ, of God's generous and forgiving love that is ours for the taking every day. As the psalmist writes, this is a love that is kind and merciful, slow to anger, full of compassion. Always. In the face of suffering, injustice, and exclusion, upon receipt of snarky social media comments and verbal assaults, in times of peace and in times of pandemic. Today's readings remind us that our response to God's goodness and mercy requires a change of heart and a commitment to ongoing conversion. To "live and die for the Lord" (Rom 14:8) not only involves agapic love, like the selflessness celebrated on *Some Good News*, it also involves forgiveness—like being open to the grace of forgiving our worst enemies. Oof, this last one seems so hard and demanding.

But we're not alone. Down through the centuries, week after week, the good news of the gospel has been proclaimed and received. God's grace enters into human hearts. It transforms. It shapes us into a beloved people capable of putting God's love *and* forgiveness into action. Two illustrations come to mind.

Three years ago this month, while serving in prison ministry, I met with a small group of women in a local prison
chapel for a communion service on this same Twenty-fourth
Sunday in Ordinary Time. After I offered a few words to unpack the parable of the unforgiving servant, the women
shared their own thoughts about the first reading and the
gospel. It didn't take long for me to realize that these women
had more to teach me than I had to offer them about seeing
ourselves as loved sinners. From where they sat, Jesus's response to Peter and the story of the merciful king offered a
priceless gift that could not and had not come from anyone
else: cancellation of their debt, freedom from the failures of
their past, a chance to begin again. During the prayers of the
faithful, I was moved by their petitions for each other, for
their families and children, for the judges who would hear
their cases, and for the corrections officers who held so much
power over their daily lives. And as they listened to and sang
along with their favorite hymn, "Amazing Grace," I prayed
too, that the communities to which they returned—my own
included—would be as forgiving as these women needed
them to be in order to rebuild their lives.

The second example concerns John Lewis. A few weeks
after his death, I listened to a replay of a 2013 *On Being* interview in which Lewis spoke with Krista Tippett about the
importance of his faith during the Civil Rights Movement, the
influence of Jesus, whom he referred to as the Great Teacher,
and the example of Mahatma Gandhi. Peaceful resistance to
violence was unnatural, he said, and not something that
everyone in the movement supported. Participation required
disciplined preparation and training. To sustain their commitment to peaceful nonviolence for the long haul, they had to
practice this "love in action," through social drama, not only
as a tactic but as a way of life. As they met with relentless hatred and oppression, their own beloved community of pro-

testers became a source of courage, strength, friendship, and even joy. They lived, he said, *as if* their goals for the wider society had already become a reality. At one point in the interview, Lewis imagined: "What would the halls of Congress be like, if we were all more comfortable saying, 'I love you, I forgive you?'"

Seventy times seven? Really? Jesus knew that we needed practice. With hearts opened wide to the amazing grace of God's mercy, can we trust that Jesus's instruction is a sign of solidarity with the human condition? Can we live *as if* it is a piece of wise advice that shapes and sustains our prophetic practice of love *and* forgiveness for the long haul? Some good news? I'd say it's the very best.

Twenty-fifth Sunday in Ordinary Time

Living in the image of God's reign

FRANCINE CARDMAN

Isaiah 55:6–9
Psalm 145:2–3, 8–9, 17–18
Philippians 1:2c–24, 27a
Matthew 20:1–16a

"What is the kingdom of heaven like?" Jesus asks in today's gospel. It is the question at the heart of his preaching: *What is the kingdom of God like?* What, that is to say, is *God* like? What happens when *God* reigns?

In Matthew's Gospel, the parable of the workers in the vineyard is preceded and followed by stories of the disciples' obtuseness in their expectations of greatness and honor. Jesus meets their desires with two jolting rejoinders: "Many who are first will be last, and the last will be first"; "Whoever wishes to be great among you must be your servant." The disciples can imagine a kingdom, but only one along the lines of empire and exclusion, power and prestige. Today's gospel calls us instead to look and listen beyond the pattern of "this world's" limitations of heart and imagination. It calls us, not to leave the world and be free of its cares and needs, but to live *here and now* in the image of God's reign.

197

To live in that image, to embody its presence, we must listen to today's gospel in a new way and learn to look at the world with the eye of our heart, letting it draw us into the compassion of God. To live in the image of God's reign is not to deny the very real demands of justice for workers, both those who labor in the heat of the day and those who are deemed idle, who stand on the street corner, not because they want to, but because no one has hired them. Nor can we overlook those who labor with little recompense and less recognition—who so often are women, children, the disenfranchised many.

What is the kingdom of heaven like? asks Jesus. It is like the landowner who calls workers to his vineyard, who keeps his word, pays a just wage, and confounds some of the workers with his generosity. God's reign is just *and* generous—embracing all who call upon God in the truth of their lives, in their deepest needs and hidden hopes. Yet, as Isaiah reminds us, God's ways and thoughts are so far above our own that we falter before God's gratuitous love. Like the workers hired at the first hour, we tend to view the world through a lens of self-interest that has little depth of field, that does not look much beyond ourselves and those closest to us, that does not take in the multiplicity of others who surround us or the complexities of their lives. Like those working from the beginning of the day, we expect to be paid more than those who worked only the last hour.

The workers who had been hired first were aggrieved, having expected to receive more in return for their long labor, resentful that the owner had treated them and the last group of workers alike, "mak[ing] them equal to us." Like them, we are captive to metrics and a stingy notion of merit. But, as Jesus declares, and the landowner demonstrates, "the last will be first, and the first last." God's hands are not tied to our narrow calculus of justice, God's mercy is not bounded by the limitations of our compassion. In *God's* reign, everyone works as their circumstances allow and everyone receives what they need. *All* are welcomed and cared for, all live equally from the generosity of God. And *all* deserve to share in God's goodness *now*, in the world that is the work of God's hands, in the community of life that encompasses and supports us all.

It is only through God's mercy that it is possible for us to live in the image of love. It is through that love that we forgive and are forgiven, through that love that we act mercifully and mercy is shown us. It is through that mercy that we work to restore community and mend creation. We are invited today, by Isaiah and the psalmist, to live and act in the ways and works of God: to make justice and generosity tangible, to embrace the outcast, welcome the stranger, open our hearts to the refugees at our gates. Like Paul, we can magnify Christ in our bodies with our work for the good of all. We can seek to conduct ourselves as he urges, in a way worthy of the gospel of Christ. Through God's generosity to the world, we can do the work that love demands for our sisters and brothers, for those who suffer from the meanness and terrors of our times, from the insularity of our personal and political worlds, from the selfishness and hardness of our collective hearts.

What is the kingdom of heaven like? What is God like? And what are *we* like? What happens when we live in the image of God's reign? How will we answer the question and call of today's readings? Let us pray that we open our hearts and imaginations to the generosity of God and the wideness of God's merciful kingdom—as in heaven, so now on earth; and as it will yet be, forever, in the fullness of God's love.

Twenty-sixth Sunday in Ordinary Time

Go out and work in the vineyard today

MARGE KLOOS, SC

Ezekiel 18:25–28
Psalm 25:4–5, 6–7, 8–9
Philippians 2:1–11
Matthew 21:28–32

In today's gospel, two sons are sent by their father to work in the vineyard. We hear the command: *Go out and work in the vineyard today.*

The sons' responses are fainthearted at best. Rare is the one who answers the command to go to work in the vineyard with a full-throated YES, and then actually shows up for wholehearted engagement.

By contrast to the two sons, the ones without reputation, prestige, and means were so moved by God's mercy, so intimately attuned to God's earthly mission—these precious ones—were the ones who proclaimed their YES then wholeheartedly showed up for work in the vineyard.

Today, we are a planet awakening to multiple injustices cascading into our consciousness. Our journey to the vineyard cannot be put on hold. The urgency of this moment calls us to go to work in the vineyard where the weeds of hate and indifference choke the vitality of our souls.

The journey to the vineyard requires us to leave behind our real or imagined security, comfort, and control.

Once we arrive in the vineyard, we're likely to be confronted with an unresponsive, hard, rocky ground into which our seeds cannot be easily sown and are even at times rejected.

An ancient Navajo proverb reminds us, that "a rocky vineyard does not need a prayer but a pickax."

Our world today needs us to pick up the pickax of compassion. By choosing the transforming work of relationship healing and tending, we chip away the boulders of hate and neglect that smother the tender shoots of unity.

We don't go to the vineyard to chisel it in our image. We go to compassionately participate in the creative energy of God, in whose image we all have been given life.

Our compassion needs to be practical and inclusive. So we might ask ourselves: Whose inner resources, long ignored, need to be heard and embraced at this time? Can we find the collective humility to relinquish oversight of the vineyard to these precious, patient others? How do we listen to the pain, the hopes, the vision, the despair, of those who've not mattered?

National Public Radio recently covered a story about a beloved doctor in the Phoenix area who died of COVID-19 at the age of ninety-nine. Jose Gabriel Lopez is being remembered for having given his life to care for people living in extreme poverty.

As a young man he left his life in Guadalajara, Mexico, and went to Arizona, fully committed to his yes. There he provided medical care for low-income families. One of the very few Spanish-speaking medical doctors in the Southwest, Dr. Lopez could have chosen a life of comfort and prestige.

Instead, he spent his talents working in the vineyard of cultural marginalization and poverty. He never asked how many more patients waited at the door. He provided non-stop medical care for generations until he was eighty-nine.

Like Dr. Lopez, we too must go to the vineyard of the world, embracing it as it is. When the Body of Christ says YES to the work that awaits us in the vineyard, we most certainly will find ourselves knee-deep in the troubles and sufferings of precious others.

In our vineyard today, the sin of racism is destroying the integrity of our humanity. In the vineyard of our relationships, what must we change about our biases, our own insecurities, our limited understanding of what it means to be human?

Why do we settle for a world in which shame and deprivations of every sort are justified?

"Go out and work in the vineyard today." Feel this command within your own skin.

The vineyard is the place of communion, the place where mercy, healing, justice, and equality consume the destructive, choking weeds of relational sin.

"Go out and work in the vineyard today . . . go with the attitude of Christ."

Take the path God opens before you. Believe that as living grace you can enter the vineyard as renewing justice and reconciling love.

Go because your integrity will grind down the rocks smothering the vines.

Go because the desperate cries for justice from every corner must be heard by a tender heart . . . your heart.

Go because shame casts shadows into our collective consciousness with unrelenting cruelty.

Go because the web of life into which we are woven is fraying and knotting into tangles of ungodly complexity caused by human excess and unholy desire.

Go with the humility of pick-axed rock, a particle of grace through which roots can burrow deeply and shoots can grow toward sunlight.

Go with the simplicity of one whose intimacy with God is visible to a hurting world.

Go with the consciousness of God's justice, God's fairness, God's integrity.

Go with open arms as the incarnation of Christ's love for our world.

Twenty-seventh Sunday in Ordinary Time

What type of tenant am I?

YUDITH PEREIRA RICO, RJM

Isaiah 5:1–7
Psalm 80:9, 12, 13–14, 15–16, 19–20
Philippians 4:6–9
Matthew 21:33–43

How is God involved in our reality, and what is our responsibility in it?

We receive the parable of the tenants from Jesus, who addresses it to the elders and the priests, the guides and pastors of the people. With it he is offering us a mirror we can use to reflect on our own lives. To the degree to which we are open, we can receive the personal message he has for us.

The characters of the parable are clearly presented.

God Himself is the landlord, says the prophet Isaiah. God is the owner, the one who created and planted the vineyard, who entrusts it to the care of the tenants, so it can grow and produce abundant fruit.

He is always present, continuously sending tenants. Jesus goes further and adds that the Son himself will be sent, and will be killed. He is revealing who he is, and also anticipating the paschal mystery we celebrate in the Eucharist.

The psalm tells us that the vineyard is the house of Israel, God's people. In the Old Testament, it was restricted to the descendants of the patriarchs, but Jesus himself extended it to all humanity, and so does the Church after him. We all, as human beings, are the vineyard, God's own property.

Jesus describes in detail the tenants and their actions.

Those tenants, today, are also ourselves. We are the ones to whom God entrusts creation and we experience it in our daily life.

We can all recognize what we have received to take care of, and to which we give our life day after day: our family, our community, our work and mission, special values and properties, and all the good things that fill our lives with sense.

The parable denounces the attitudes of the elders and the priests.

Like the tenants, they want to become the landlords and owners at any price.

The root of their behavior is their ambition, their desire for ownership of reality. They don't recognize their own responsibility or their accountability to the Lord. They manipulate and invert the relations within the vineyard: appropriation instead of return, aggression in the place of care, and death instead of life.

This leads them to greed. They are closed in on their own being and enthrone themselves as their own lord. They value only their own existence. Neither the vineyard, nor the other employees, nor the landlord nor his son count.

We too can have such attitudes as a result of what Pope Francis calls "mundanization"—being closed in on one's self, concerned solely with our own small realities and worries, living only to fulfill our own happiness, using every means for it, mindful of nothing else.

We can ask ourselves:

What type of tenant am I? Do I live to serve and to take care of others, or do I use them for my own profit and interest? Do I feel responsible and am I conscious of my accountability for all I have received?

With his parable, Jesus shows the dramatic consequences of the ambition, greed, and closedness of the tenants.

As we look around at our world, we see the misuse of the Earth's resources for the profit of a small group, the blood of our brothers and sisters killed by violence and wars. Such things involve us all.

Let us allow the parable to open our eyes to a bigger scene: God entrusts to us not only our small reality but the whole of creation, and every human being in it, all of whom are our brothers and sisters. He calls us to serve and to be responsible for them. We cannot close our eyes or avoid our responsibility with the excuse that we are focused on our particular situations and worries.

The cry of the people of South Sudan is an example of how actual this parable is. South Sudan is a vineyard where a silent genocide is taking place before the eyes of the world; where its leaders are fighting for power and benefiting their own families and tribes with the land's resources; where the international community is taking a two-sided attitude, sending aid but providing the weapons for the ongoing war, leaving the multinationals to benefit from the chaotic situation by uncontrolledly extracting primary resources. Meanwhile, people are being raped and killed; they are starving and displaced.

The failure of the youngest country in the world is the responsibility of all.

The Son of God is really dying in each child, man, and woman. The Son of God is displaced in each of the two million people who have abandoned their homes; agonizing in each person who is starving and sick; assaulted in each girl and woman who suffers rape as a weapon of war. The Son is actualizing his passion and resurrection in each victim under the world's blindness.

Pope Francis denounces our avoidance of responsibility and gives it a name—the globalization of indifference. This is the action of Evil in our world, in us, because of our personal lack of action.

At this point we can consider:

*Are these situations affecting my sensitivity and
personal, political, and social choices?*

*Am I conscious of the personal situations behind the
figures and statistics?*

We believe that as disciples and followers of Jesus we are responsible for our brothers and sisters.

Are my actions witnessing that faith?

What does the Lord want to tell us with his parable?

What will he ask us when our lives here end?

Twenty-eighth Sunday in Ordinary Time

Accepting the invitation to the feast

PETRA DANKOVA

Isaiah 25:6–10a
Psalm 23:1–3a, 3b–4, 5, 6
Philippians 4:12–14, 19–20
Matthew 22:1–14

I wrestled with today's readings, and the experience reminded me of Jacob fighting with God at the Jabbok. Sometimes we have to struggle—with God, with the Bible, with our Church.

Today, first we hear the beautiful account in Isaiah of a feast prepared for us by God, then Saint Paul's heartening words about a faith that endures in all circumstances . . . and then there is the gospel—a parable of a generous invitation to a feast, an invitation that some ignore. And those who refuse are punished in really gruesome ways. The last verse tops it all: Many are invited but few are chosen. What are we to do with that? How can we soften the meaning of this verse?

Sure, we could ignore it, we could just take the shorter version of the reading and pretend that the hard-hitting verses are not there at all. But I suspect that is not how we discover our God, a God who invites us to take off a veil: an "intransparency" that covers the true nature of things! We have to stick with the text. We have to stick with all our questions. We have to struggle, and we know that somewhere in there God can be found.

To stick with it is a feeling I know well! My partner and I are asked all the time why we stick with the Catholic Church. Isn't that a terrible place to be a same-sex couple? Sometimes that's true. And we cannot gloss over these moments, these painful parts of our experience with the Catholic Church. But in the same way, we cannot deny that our Church is a life-giving place of beautiful encounters and really transformative experiences. And I, as someone who converted to Catholicism, have really been invited to this feast—to the table of the Eucharist and to the community of the Church—and I cannot just walk away from that.

I imagine that not only LGBTQ Catholics but many of us feel that sometimes the Church is a place where we are very well fed and sometimes it's a place where we go hungry. Saint Paul in today's second reading tells us that we can bear that when we are centered on God, centered on the one who strengthens us in all circumstances.

I think that Saint Paul has another lesson for us. He shows us that, just like him, it helps us when someone notices, when someone "shares in our distress."

A couple of months ago, Germany debated and ultimately approved a law allowing same-sex marriage. At the time, what stung me the most from Church officials was not their defending the "traditional view of a family"—after all, I know that the debate as it took place in Germany was quite polite and open and really constructive. What stung me was one official who declared that discussing same-sex marriage so much is really not appropriate because it is a marginal issue that doesn't deserve so much attention. That hurt—because I think it sums up so clearly what many LGBTQ persons and families and many others experience in our Church: this feeling of being unimportant, of being disregarded, of being expendable. We are reduced to a hotly debated issue and the humanity of us gets lost in the process. Under the defense of a doctrine, the lived experience of people for whom getting married is a major life experience and a decision that shapes their lives—that is lost.

What different, positive experience I have had with my family, our friends, the pastoral workers in our parish and our diocese who have taken the time to get to know me and my partner and who have really shared in our joys and in our distress. There, together, we have had a glimpse of the heavenly feast where the veil is lifted and we see that we are all children of God, are all fed by God's love. A pastoral worker recently told me: "In the Church I serve, there has to be a place for everyone to come as they are, without having to hide or distort any part of themselves." That is our Church at its best and that is a glimpse of heaven on earth.

I cannot tell you that I am fully reconciled with today's readings, or with the Church as it is today. I can only invite you to wrestle with it. And to stick with it. And to use your faith to guide you to accept the invitation to the feast. Accept it, despite not being able to understand every detail of the picture, every word of the text. It is the encounter and our desire to know the distress of each other that will help us to arrive at this heavenly feast.

I leave you with two movements of a prayer by German Jesuit Peter Koester: "My life is a bowl, ready to receive and ready to give. God, make stronger what brings me closer to you and help me to recognize what takes me away from you. Help me to bear the tension between what is and what is not yet, between desire and fulfillment. Amen."

Twenty-ninth Sunday in Ordinary Time

Letting go of our idols

KATHERINE A. GREINER

Isaiah 45:1, 4–6
Psalm 96:1, 3, 4–5, 7–8, 9–10
1 Thessalonians 1:1–5b
Matthew 22:15–21

One of my favorite lines of poetry comes from the last line of Mary Oliver's poem, "A Summer's Day." Oliver writes, "Tell me, what do you plan to do with your one wild and precious life?"

This line hits me like a sucker punch to the gut. The blunt question uncovers a deep, uncomfortable truth that sometimes the life I'm leading is not the life I want to live. I get so distracted striving for that which will not sustain, spending my time and energy chasing affirmation and accolades, financial stability, job security, success that I forget my center, I lose sight of my center, my true desires. It is not that things like financial stability and affirmation are bad in and of themselves. But they don't always deliver the life I truly desire. Oliver's blunt question reminds me to return to the center of my being, to remember that all we have is the gift of life and we are called to live it to the fullest. The line refocuses my attention to that center within me that yearns for communion with God, with others, and with myself.

In today's gospel, we hear Jesus deliver a similar blow to the Pharisees. Attempting to entrap Jesus, they pose a trick question. Pay the census tax, or not? If Jesus says, "Yes, pay it!" He could be accused of idolatry. Had he said "No," Jesus could have put himself at the mercy of Roman law. Jesus does neither. Rather, he turns the question back to the Pharisees. "Show me the coin," he says. In doing so, he reveals their hypocrisy. There it is, the coin, stamped with Caesar's image and drawn from their own pockets.

"Whose image is on this coin?"

"Caesar's," they respond.

We can almost see the squirming, the aversion of eyes. And then, here it comes, "Then repay to Caesar what is Caesar's and to God what belongs to God."

Far from an economics lesson or even a lecture on civic duty, this story—along with the other readings for today—is about our identity, specifically, our identity in God. We belong to God. When we understand the truth of that reality, we see life as gift, precious and wild, meant to be poured out on that which matters: gratitude, service, beauty, truth, mercy, love. Life is not meant to be spent fearfully gathering up trappings that our culture claims we need. Life is not to be hoarded; rather, it is meant to be poured out.

This story is a familiar riff on the repeated gospel theme: Jesus comes that we may have life and have it abundantly. Even more so, Jesus comes to show us *that we have life* and *how to live it abundantly.* Jesus's courage comes from his deep abiding faith that he belongs to God. He believes to the depth of his core the words spoken at his baptism: "You are my beloved." Living out of this reality, Jesus pours himself out, expends his energy on healing the sick, feeding the hungry, comforting the afflicted, the sorrowful, the forgotten. His single-minded confidence in God's love even takes him to his death. But it also brings forth resurrection and new life.

Jesus' admonition in today's gospel calls the Pharisees to claim the truth that they too belong to God. He reminds them that their identity is not defined by the coins hidden away in their pockets but rather by the love of God in their hearts. Jesus urges them to let go of the trappings of idolatry, all that keeps them from spending their lives on what matters.

For those of us in positions of privilege and power, Jesus's words should cut us to the core. This gospel reveals our own pharisaical tendencies and reminds us that we are not the money in our bank account. We are not our jobs. Our identities run much deeper than our national borders, than our political parties, than our religious affiliations. When we cling to the security that is offered by these dangerous idols, we become distracted at best, violent at worst. Just as the Pharisees carried Caesar's image in their pockets, we can become complicit in the very structures of sin we claim to abhor. Letting go of these idols frees us to embrace our shared vulnerability and to live out of the confidence that we belong to God.

There is no doubt that this takes immense courage. People who possess such courage resist the idols of power and prestige and economic success. They are centered in a place of deep freedom and joy, hope and wisdom. They are prophets in our midst, usually living quite ordinary lives. Like Jesus, they encourage us to empty our pockets of burdensome and harmful idols and fix our attention on the abiding Spirit of Life creatively laboring in and through us. Like Jesus, they assure us that first and foremost we belong to God. Through their courageous witness, they ask us, "Tell me, what will you do with your one wild and precious life?"

Thirtieth Sunday in Ordinary Time

Journeying with traveling Jesus

PAULINE HOVEY

Exodus 22:20–26
Psalm 18:2–3, 3–4, 47, 51
1 Thessalonians 1:5c–10
Matthew 22:34–40

I will surely hear their cry.

For I have loved them with an everlasting love. Just as I love you. There is no separation in my heart.

This is how I hear God speak in this morning's readings. God, who hears the cries of the afflicted, the oppressed, the abused, the brokenhearted. God, who hears the cries of the suffering widows, the aliens on unfamiliar soil.

How I detest that word: aliens.

I have heard it so often with such negative connotations. To demean, to inflict hatred and prejudice toward an entire group of people.

But the definition of alien simply is *"one belonging to a foreign country or nation."*

And all of us know someone to whom that term applies— whether it's grandparents, like mine, who were once aliens in this country, or the Jesus we worship who had no place to lay his head, born in Bethlehem of Judea, raised in Nazareth of

Galilee. Drifter along the seacoast towns of Capernaum and Magdala. Where did he belong?

Over these past several years I've come to know this traveling Jesus much more intimately, as I myself became the widow looking for a new place to lay her head. And most especially as I recognized his presence in the foreigners I accompanied at our southern border.

You see, for about five years I volunteered at houses of hospitality in El Paso where we received refugees and asylum-seekers, so-called aliens vetted and released to us by ICE (immigration and customs enforcement). Most of them were from the countries of Honduras, El Salvador, and Guatemala. We accompanied these weary travelers on their journey to their family sponsors, to a place of safety, temporary freedom, and the hope of life without the constant threat of rape, extortion, harm to their children or themselves.

My fellow volunteers and I—who included people from both the greater El Paso community and from all over the country—accompanied our guests with kindness and compassion and with the dignity and respect all human beings deserve. And they sometimes began to feel safe and relaxed enough to share their stories.

There were many widows among them. Strong women whose husbands had been murdered—sometimes in front of them—and, try as they might, they couldn't support their children when constantly being extorted by a local gang. Your money or your daughter. That was the usual threat.

So they would flee their homeland, taking very few possessions, if any.

But here's the thing: these foreigners traveling with nothing or next to nothing—they were the imitators of Christ to me!—the ones Paul refers to in his First Letter to the Thessalonians in today's second reading. These people—both women and men—had received the word of God in great affliction, under terrible duress, nonexistent options, enduring cruel judgments and treatment along the way. Yet they carried the joy of the Holy Spirit within them, to us and to one another. Their faith journeyed with them.

They were—and are—the model for all believers that Paul speaks of. I can say that because of the effect they had on me and on my fellow volunteers. They enabled me to understand the meaning of the two greatest commandments Jesus teaches us to follow. To love the Lord your God with all your heart, with all your soul, with all your mind and all your strength. And to love your neighbor as yourself.

How do I love my neighbor *as* myself? I came to understand that the kind of love Jesus is talking about doesn't have the restrictions or boundaries we so often put on loving others.

This love is extravagant. It is loving without distinction, without placing conditions on worthiness or place of origin.

Let me give you a couple of examples:

One of our volunteer drivers was taking several mothers and their children from our shelter to the bus station so they could travel on to their family sponsors. One of the women asked our driver if she could stop to exchange money. She told our driver she had twenty dollars and wanted change so she could give half of it to the woman she was traveling with—a woman she didn't know: "I want to give her ten dollars because I have twenty dollars and she has nothing."

It's not an isolated incident. We witnessed this kind of generosity many times.

Our director of Annunciation House often tells similar stories. Once his house of hospitality had taken in a woman who was ill, and when she got better, she agreed to take on a day of housekeeping from someone who'd called looking for a day laborer. When the woman returned to the house after a long day of housecleaning, she had been given only fifteen dollars for her full day's work. She gave ten dollars to our director to put aside for her and then she gave him the remaining five dollars and told him to give it to someone who needed it more than she did.

Whenever I witness or hear about exchanges like this, I feel as though I am living in another world.

Who does this? Who gives half of what they have to a stranger? Or one-third of what they've earned when they don't even know when they will next receive any income?

Who does this? Imitators of Christ.

Such actions make no sense in "our" world with its desire for security and certainty. But in Jesus's world of reckless, extravagant love, these actions are life-giving. And my "alien" brothers and sisters understand that.

They understand the greatest commandment, and what it means to say *the second one is like it.* For to love you neighbor *AS yourself* means to know there is no separation between us. Just as there is no separation in God's heart. Every one of us carries the Divine within us and therefore can never be separated from the love of God.

Thank God they carried that awareness of who they are and how loved they are. Because they endured such cruelty. And still do.

Yes, the alien, the stranger, taught me what it means to be an imitator of Christ.

And, in meeting them and accompanying them, I understand why God says: "*I will surely hear their cry.*"

Thirty-first Sunday
in Ordinary Time

Created to be Christ for others

TERRY BATTAGLIA

Malachi 1:14b–2:2b, 8–10
Psalm 131:1, 2, 3
1 Thessalonians 2:7b–9, 13
Matthew 23:1–12

The focus of our readings today is on mission and love. In Matthew's Gospel, Jesus instructs his followers to boldly proclaim to others: "To live as we do, act as we do." Those are bold words; what do they mean? They mean living a life of service of love and forgiveness. Matthew is not clumsy when he illustrates this in his Gospel. He is deliberate; he is thoughtful; he says clearly what we are to do. We are to offer ourselves up as sacrifice for another, as servants to one another.

Paul's First Letter to the Thessalonians instructs his followers to live by the words of Christ by giving their very lives—their very beings. They are to offer themselves as a living sacrifice in the world, to be Christ for others, to live a life of service and of love.

There's a story told of a woman who works downtown. She spends every day in an office and at lunchtime goes downstairs and across the street to her favorite lunch place. It is in a downtown metropolitan area, so there are always several homeless people on the street corner begging for money.

On one particular day, she was in a bit of a foul mood as she was going down the stairs and heading for the door. Once she got outside, she saw a mother and her young child begging for money. Her reaction was rage—and anger with God. Silently she said: "God! Why why do you allow this to happen? How can you allow children to be homeless and hungry? Why don't you do something about this?" Immediately a voice came back to her and said, "I did. I created you."

I think that is the message of the gospel. We are created to be Christ in the world today. We are created to be Christ for others, to live the gospel not just with our words, but with our actions.

Thirty-second Sunday in Ordinary Time

The oil of justice and mercy

PATRICIA SMITH, RSM

Wisdom 6:12–16
Psalm 63:2, 3–4, 5–6, 7–8
1 Thessalonians 4:13–18
Matthew 25:1–13

When I saw the gospel for this Sunday, I thought, "Oh great! What do I do with this?" Here is another occasion, among so many in the ancient world, where females appear ditzy and not very responsible. What can we overlook as a product of its time? What can we take away from today's parable?

To understand what is going on in our gospel, we have to recall something about our ancestors in the Christian faith. For years following Jesus's death and resurrection, his followers lived with the active hope that he would return to them soon. The risen Christ would gather the elect, call them to account for their lives, and truly establish the reign of God. So, they were preoccupied with living appropriately during this time of waiting for his return. Now, waiting for anything is always a time of uncertainty. But, just as we live in such a time today, so did they, asking themselves, "How are we to live now—with more questions than answers, more change than stability, more unknowns than knowns?" The entire gospel, both before and after our passage, is about the proper response to that question. How are we to live now?

The setting of our parable is that of the wedding custom at the time of Jesus. Bridesmaids (young girls often age twelve or thirteen) waited with a bride for her intended groom, who would come to her father's house to negotiate the terms of the marriage contract. The role of the bridesmaids was to welcome the groom and, after the completion of the negotiation, escort the couple to the groom's house for a big feast. Jesus makes the point of the parable clear: all are to live in constant vigilance, lest they be caught off guard by the groom's arrival. Even if they doze off, the bridesmaids are expected to be ready to perform their welcoming role, because they would have filled their lamps with oil.

But wait. Here half of the bridesmaids are fully prepared to light their lamps and lead the procession. The other half have to find an open 7-Eleven. Now, in the culture of that time, "oil" was more than a means to light lamps. It was a symbol for good works, especially the good works of justice and mercy. That is why this chapter in Matthew ends with the words, "I was hungry and you gave me food," and so forth. The groom's refusal to let the foolish five into the party is echoed later in Matthew 25, where those who did not give food to the hungry, drink to the thirsty, and so on cannot enter into eternal life. The oil of good works is the key to entering the reign of God.

I need to stop here and speculate, thinking beyond what happens in our story. I wonder why the five wise bridesmaids couldn't have shared some of their oil (some of their good works). That would have been an appropriate response to what had happened in Jesus's ministry with the feeding of the five thousand. They could have multiplied the goodness rather than keeping it for themselves. They could have broadened the whole experience of community support for the couple. But I guess that would have missed the point of the story. Which is: life presents us with lots of unknowns. We need to always be ready for them. The poet Maya Angelou puts it this way: *"Hoping for the best, prepared for the worst, and unsurprised by anything in between."*

In their own time, Matthew's audience were ardently awaiting the final coming, the end of the world as they knew it. As that didn't happen, later generations transferred the hope of Christ's coming to the individual's own personal life at the moment of death. "You know not the day nor the hour." I suggest returning to the original practice. Thomas Merton puts it well. He says, "The great historical event, the coming of the Kingdom is made clear and is 'realized' in proportion as Christians live the life of the Kingdom in the circumstances of their own place and time." And so, in each and every moment, we must be ever vigilant to practice good works, especially justice, mercy, and all the blessings so critically needed in our world today. You know what they are.

On another note, I was happy to see that the poetry of our first reading contrasts with the negative image of the five foolish bridesmaids. The poem praises the beautiful image of Wisdom—a feminine image, a "she." This title presents an alternative to the exclusively patriarchal language about God—like father, warrior, king. At its deepest level, Wisdom is a female symbol for the very mystery of God. She is the personification of God's presence and activity in the created world. She guides God's creatures along the right path in life. She delights in human beings. She is God's creative energy, involved with the world.

This first reading introduces the gospel's themes of light and watchfulness. Wisdom is eminently attractive and attracting (resplendent). She is near us (sitting by our side, making her rounds). She is gracious, appearing everywhere to those who seek her. Taking Wisdom seriously provides new images of the Holy One, especially (though not exclusively) welcomed by many women and girls today. May we be ever watchful for these images. May Wisdom open our eyes to the power of God's gracious, patient love already enveloping us in her open arms today.

Thirty-third Sunday in Ordinary Time

Using our God-given talents

RITA L. HOULIHAN

Proverbs 31:10–13, 19–20, 30–31
Psalm 128:1–2, 3, 4–5
1 Thessalonians 5:1–6
Matthew 25:14–30

"Of those who have received much, much is expected": this was one of my mother's favorite mantras. It was a guiding force in our family—our gifts are to be shared, to help bring about the kingdom of God here on earth. Matthew's series of parables of the kingdom these past few weeks urge us to prepare, to be wise, and in today's parable, not to hoard.

There are different interpretations of this parable of the "talents." In one it is a mandate for all of us to develop our unique talents. I grew up with that version.

In another interpretation, the master is not God and the first two servants simply trade money in unspecified deals to make their master richer and richer. Barbara Reid suggests that a first-century Jewish audience would have seen the last servant, the one who hid the talent, as the hero—one who refused to participate in a system that glorifies making money over all else.

224

So I must ask, "Did someone lose out in the deals the first two servants made?" Our gifts are not to be used to take advantage of others. And why does this master have to be so rich? Does the last servant's punishment warn us it is risky to stand for a more human-centered system in which money and work produce the essentials—food, shelter, clothing, art—without hoarding? This interpretation paints a picture of what we need to do to be fully present in the kingdom of God and to avoid the devastating effects of rigid capitalism in which accumulating money is the goal versus productive capitalism with the goal of creating life-giving products and services. This interpretation carries a most essential message for us today.

But I need to go back to my earliest memories of this parable. The first time I would have heard it was November 1970. It, and our first reading from Proverbs 31, were part of the new Year A lectionary. As a college senior I was struggling with what to do with my life. I heard the word "talents" and my mother's mantra came to mind. (I now know "talents" was a quantity of money in the first century—I did not know that back in 1970.) It was comforting to know that my mission was straightforward—find and use my talents. It didn't overwhelm me as much as always being kind and generous—it seemed more doable to find a talent and use it. The parable drew me in and kept me searching. Later my mandate would expand to appreciating the gifts of others and helping children develop theirs.

Which takes us to our first reading, the Woman of Worth of Proverbs 31. Our children need to know this Woman of Worth—*Esheth Ayil* [phonetic translation]. Most translations identify her as a "worthy wife" but the Hebrew is "woman" (there is no word for "wife" in Hebrew). The proverb is an acrostic with the first letter of each couplet a letter of the Hebrew alphabet. Scholars speculate that it was used to teach girls to read and that women who gathered in circles to learn business would have listened to it while others formed networks of weavers. We need to bring this Woman of Worth with all her talents and joys to our children today.

There is a chilling moment in a recent documentary on sex trafficking when a sheriff in Chicago asks a trafficker, "How do you find the girls?" Surprisingly, he answers, "I go to the malls. When I see a girl alone, even just for a few minutes, I go up and say, 'You have beautiful eyes.' If she looks at me and says, 'Thank you' I move on. If she looks down and is unsure, I know I have a chance." Our children need to know this Woman of Valor and Strength, to see her using her talents for good and to know they can do the same. We need to dig to find her talents—our lectionary omits sixteen verses, burying praise for her capabilities, hard work, business acumen, generosity, and love of God's law of kindness.

In the missing verses we learn that she clothes her family in crimson so they "do not fear the cold," she assesses her estate and buys choice land, she plants a vineyard and feeds her family, she spins wool and flax and makes sashes to sell in the market. She opens her mouth and the Torah, the law of kindness comes forth. Her children and her husband rise up to praise her. Some see the husband leaving all the work to his capable wife—but we can also see her commitment to use all of her gifts to care for her family, herself, and her community. Reading the missing verses I found a sense of delight pouring off the pages as one gift after another emerged.

Her enterprises remind me of a number of New Testament women—Lydia of Philippi, the head of a cloth-dyeing business and founder, with Paul, of the Church at Philippi; Prisca, who with her husband Aquila was a tent maker and founded several Christian communities; and the disciples from Galilee—Mary Magdalene, Joanna, and Susanna—women of means who supported Jesus in his ministry. Perhaps these women heard and heeded the advice of their ancestor, this "Worthy Woman" of Proverbs 31.

We adults need to be this woman of worth and integrity more than ever today. Imagine if all our daughters and sons saw themselves in her and imagine if they received the "Torah of kindness" from our lips. She certainly used every one of her God-given talents and more. It's a shame so much is omitted from this Sunday's reading.

To get to know the full Woman of Worth, treat yourself to reading and sharing all of Proverbs 31. Now let us pray— "Give her a share in the fruit of her hands, and let her works praise her in the city gates."

SOLEMNITIES AND FEASTS

Immaculate Conception
of the Blessed Virgin Mary

Free to choose

Barbara E. Reid, OP

Genesis 3:9–15, 20
Psalm 98:1, 2–3ab, 3cd–4
Ephesians 1:3–6, 11–12
Luke 1:26–38

As a child I loved the feast of the Immaculate Conception because we had the day off from school! And we had wonderful
traditions in our family of going Christmas shopping and baking cookies on that day. And as a budding perfectionist, I
loved the image of the perfect Virgin Mary who had no stain
of sin, even from her very conception. I had a milk-bottle theology—I imagined our souls as pure white milk bottles, but
then they got all splotched with dark stains of sin (I know, the
metaphor breaks down here!). Confession, as we called the
sacrament of reconciliation in those days, would wipe away all
the blotches and return us to that pure white milk-bottle state
again. I pictured Mary as never having to deal with any
blotches, being in a special category all her own, never having
to deal with life's difficulties and temptations and tough decisions like we did. Sure, she suffered, especially seeing her son

brutally executed, but I envisioned her life as being so different from mine, from ours.

Vatican II set us on a different path for how to relate to Mary, for which I am deeply grateful. Seeing her as one like us, first among disciples, put a human face on her and situated her right in our midst, modeling for us how we, too, can learn how to be faithful to God in the midst of all kinds of difficulties and struggles and challenges.

Today's first reading gives us a mythical explanation for why life is so difficult, why there are tensions between us—"enmity" between humans and other creatures. The verses that follow today's lesson from Genesis describe how all areas of life are adversely affected by human sin—God's dream for creation has been tarnished by the refusal of human beings to accept and participate fully in the extraordinary love and creative energy poured out on us.

But the gospel reading and today's feast lift us out of the mire of our sinfulness and invite us once again to allow ourselves to be touched and transformed by God's grace and mercy, extended to us in the most extraordinary moments on ordinary days. Mary shows us how to respond.

It seems to have been just an ordinary day in Nazareth. Mary was making wedding plans when God's messenger came, asking of her what seemed to be impossible. This annunciation story is very much like other annunciation stories in the Bible, where Sarah, Hagar, Samson's mother, and Mary's relative Elizabeth are chosen by God to give birth in seemingly impossible situations to a son who will bring God's liberating work to a new climax.

But the annunciation to Mary is also very much like the call of a prophet. In the call stories of Moses, Jeremiah, Amos, and Isaiah, we can see the same dynamics. The call usually happens in the midst of ordinary, everyday life, as it did for Moses, tending his flock. And the first reaction is fear.

The angelic messenger gives a reassurance: Do not be afraid; God's grace, God's favor is with you. And then the angel tells the prophet what God wants them to do—it is usually a mission impossible, like: "I will send you to Pharaoh to bring my people, the Israelites, out of Egypt" (Exod 3:10). True prophets always object—Moses that he wasn't good at speaking; Jeremiah that he was too young; Isaiah that he had unclean lips; Mary that she "does not know man." And God always has a way around the objection. To Jeremiah, "Do not be afraid, I am with you" (Jer 1:8); for Moses, God will appoint his brother and sister, who are good with words, to prophesy with him; for Isaiah, a burning coal takes care of the unclean lips! (Isa 6:6–7); for Mary, "nothing is impossible with God."

In prophetic call stories, the divine messenger gives a reassurance and oftentimes a sign: "Do not be afraid"; "the Holy Spirit will come upon you and the power of the Most High will overshadow you." Concrete signs include a bush that burns and is not consumed, and an impossible pregnancy for a cousin who is far past the age of childbearing. God's grace and mercy are what will enable the prophet to accomplish the extraordinarily difficult mission entrusted to them. But God will never force anyone.

The angel waits.... Holy Wisdom holds her breath.... Will Mary say yes? Will we?

"Here am I, the servant of the Lord; let it be done to me according to your word."

Opening herself to God's enlivening, creative, unpredictable power, she says "Yes" to she knows not what; "Yes" not to God's favor only upon her but upon all humankind and all creation. She says she is God's "servant,"—literally "slave," *doulē* in Greek—and asserts, "Let it be done to me according to your word."

And here I choke.

I hear her words as able to be used to keep people who are in detestable servile positions, firmly mired there, with divine approbation. When so many women have been "done unto" according to men's wills, in so many abusive ways, I find myself choking on those words. So many times I have seen and heard Mary's response being used to reinforce passivity, docility, subservience for women. Never have I heard preachers encourage women to emulate Mary's fierce denunciation of injustices and her bold proclamation of God's mercy that lifts up all the humiliated and fills all the hungry, lowering all the mighty and overfed, as we have in Mary's Magnificat.

A way forward may be to hear Mary's assent to Gabriel as that of an empowered woman who is entirely free to choose, who asserts that God is the one she will serve, and no one else. Her service is not imposed on her, nor is her manner of service bound by gender stereotypes. She not only gives birth to the ultimate prophet who will free people from their sinfulness, but she herself is a prophet and a preacher of justice as she sings out her Magnificat.

As we celebrate her sinlessness, from her moment of conception, we celebrate simultaneously God's overwhelming grace and mercy, grace constantly poured out upon us, grace that cannot be undone by human sinfulness. We celebrate Mary's "Yes" to participate with her whole being in God's creative and saving work, as all of us, disciples both female and male, allow ourselves to become ever more open to and transformed by this work of the Sinless One in us.

Our Lady of Guadalupe
Accepting the mystery of God

Jutta Battenberg Galindo

Zechariah 2:14–17
Judith 13:18bcde, 19
Luke 1:39–47

Today, December twelfth, we celebrate the feast of Our Lady of Guadalupe, whose importance, in Latin American countries in general and in Mexico in particular, is undeniable. It is a devotion that has provided hope, solidarity, and strength in response to the dramatic context of oppression, confusion, and suffering caused by the conquest and the colony.

Our Lady of Guadalupe is a figure that managed to be equally significant for natives, Spanish, and Creole. Her image has served as one of the most important symbols around which the Mexican identity was built, so much so that it worked as banner in the struggle for the independence of my country.

Under the shelter of the Guadalupana, many Mexicans and Latin Americans have entrusted ourselves to her care. We have become stronger in our battles and we have sympathized with those most in need because we have accepted the mystery of God in our lives.

Indeed, precisely in this most important Marian feast for my people, I want to underline the human aspect of our Lady, because of the relationship and the meaning that this has or can have in the experiences and expressions of Catholics.

The reading of the gospel reminds us of two fundamental facts in Christian experience. First, God's initiative to reach our lives, as it came to Mary more than two thousand years ago; second, the need for the human response to accept his offer to dwell among us. For this reason, the fiat of the Virgin is so significant that, despite the legitimate disturbance due to the weird message and recognizing that, behind the words of the angel, comes something until that moment unknown and confusing, she gives a sustained "Yes" that transformed her life and the history of humankind.

Certainly, God loves us in such a way that he always searches for us, but only as a proposal, as a respectful constant invitation to receive from him the life that he gives us with full hands, but our reception of that gift depends on our free will to materialize that transformation. Therefore, it is up to us to accept the grace that comes from above and allow it to grow in us and to be delivered to the whole of humanity, without distinction, exclusion, or petty favoritism, and preferably for those most in need because of their conditions of oppression, injustice, and suffering.

Although the Father has already given us salvation through the Son in the Holy Spirit, it needs to be fulfilled through men and women who, recognizing in ourselves the wonders that God has done in our stories, commit ourselves to serving within the physical, social, economic, and cultural spaces in which we live, especially in caring for the life and future of the less favored.

The experience of recognizing and accepting that the mystery of God lives among us is a source of joy as affirmed by the reading from Zechariah, a joy that is necessarily communal and historical, that touches our lives, that humanizes our existence, that pushes us to be there for others without denying our own happiness. It is the joy which we celebrate especially on this day in the manifestation of the Guadalupana in Latin lands, the joy that is present in us and in everyone who invokes and recognizes her as a loving mother who cares, protects, and inspires us.

The responsorial, from the Book of Judith, reminds us that we are able to recognize when the mystery of God germinates and bears fruit in others. In them we recognize the light they give us, the strength they give us, the hope they give us, and the certainty of God's actions in history.

Sisters and brothers, on this feast of Our Lady of Guadalupe, I invite you to allow, as the Virgin did, the love of God to germinate in each one of us, emerge in our relationships, give strength and meaning in human history, and transform the culture of death to a full living space for everyone.

Feast of the Presentation of the Lord

Holy with hope

KATHY LILLA COX

Malachi 3:1–4
Psalm 24:7, 8, 9, 10
Hebrews 2:14–18
Luke 2:22–40

"Crisp holly with red berries—we are holy with hope," writes poet laureate Joy Harjo in her poem "Walk." "We are holy with hope." Words that stopped me short. Am I, are we, holy with hope in a world with out-of-control wildfires, devastating floods, children in cages, families in exile, corruption, abuse, and on and on? What do we hope for amidst so many horrors? Do we recognize when God answers our hopes, and especially our expectations for change and healing, if God appears in unexpected people or places?

Today's readings speak to us about expectations—preparing for them, recognizing their fulfillment, proclaiming them. Luke narrates a story demonstrating how expectations for redemption are recognized in an unexpected way. The story that begins with Mary and Joseph following Jewish law by presenting Jesus at the temple. For two elders of the Jewish community, Simeon and Anna, this ordinary, required ritual—

the presentation—revealed to them that the long-awaited Messiah had shown up, shown up in the infant Jesus.

Simeon understood that he would not die until he saw the Messiah. Upon seeing Jesus, he recognized the fulfillment of that promise, and taking the baby Jesus into his arms, blessed God. And in that blessing, Simeon moved the outreach of Jesus's future ministry not just to the Israelites but also to the Gentiles. For many churchgoers this is where the story will end, with Simeon's canticle of praise. But the lectionary has two options for today: a shorter version and a longer version that continues the presentation story. Therefore, as radio broadcaster Paul Harvey used to say, "And now for the rest of the story."

Luke continues his narrative by telling us that Mary and Joseph are amazed at Simeon's words about Jesus. This had me wondering why. Joseph's amazement I get, but Mary's? We heard during Advent that she said, "Yes, let it be done to me according to your will," when she was told she would bear the Messiah. Her amazement here points to the possibility that even Mary's fiat, like every major commitment, needs to be made again and again so that we can see anew how God is working. Maybe Mary needed Simeon's witness as much as Simeon needed to see Jesus.

Additionally, in the longer presentation story we meet Anna. Anna is easy to overlook, since Simeon seems to have the larger role, a speaking one. Paying attention to how Simeon with a speaking role proclaims Jesus as Messiah, we might miss and overlook Anna, the quieter presence who also proclaims Jesus as the Messiah.

So, who is Anna? She is named prophetess, like Miriam, Deborah, and Huldah, female prophets before her. Luke speaks to Anna's prophetic lineage which recalls prophets who see God face to face, who proclaim and announce that encounter. Anna is a widow, one of the "poor ones" of Israel who rely on God.

We know this Anna by her actions—worshiping, fasting, praying, waiting—all actions performed in the temple as she waited for the redemption of Jerusalem, as she waited to see God's revelation to God's people, waited to see God face to face and then proclaim the fulfillment of the promises made in Isaiah, promises we heard just recently in Advent.

Anna saw the fulfillment of God's promises in the infant Jesus, vulnerable and dependent on others; she saw God face to face in the vulnerability and dependence of a child, and, "she gave thanks to God and spoke about the child to all who were awaiting the redemption of Jerusalem (Luke 2:38)."

Both Simeon and Anna wait for the Messiah, recognize the Messiah, speak about him, and praise God. Both witness "the expectation of Israel fulfilled in Jesus." Simeon speaks for himself, speaks to Mary and Joseph. Anna goes and speaks to the community and whoever will listen about the infant Jesus. She proclaims God's presence in Jesus to the community.

She is older, aged like Elizabeth, Zechariah, and Simeon, none of whom probably saw the salvation and redemption that would come from the ministry of the infant Jesus, "who grew and became strong, filled with wisdom . . . (Luke 2:40)."

What does the presentation and revelation of God, as witnessed by Anna, mean for us today? Anna challenges us when we are tempted to despair and lose hope. By attending to Anna's story, we are asked if we can wait with her for an undetermined period of time Can we prepare with fasting and prayer? Can we develop a willingness to see the infancy of God's promises being incarnated into the world, a world awaiting and needing restoration, reconciliation, redemption, and peace? And then when God arrives, in persons young, vulnerable, and needing care, can we recognize that we are seeing God face to face, give thanks, and proclaim God's presence in our midst to others awaiting redemption, even as we continue to hope for God's promises to be fully realized?

Solemnity of the Most Holy Trinity

Who will teach us the steps?

ANTOINETTE GUTZLER, MM

Exodus 34:4b–6, 8–9
Daniel 3:52, 53, 54, 55, 56
2 Corinthians 13:11–13
John 3:16–18

In the 2004 movie "Shall We Dance?" there is a scene where Richard Gere (who has secretly been taking dance lessons) asks his wife, Susan Sarandon, to dance. She says, "I don't know how. I don't know the steps." To which he replies, "I'll teach you."

Now you might think that is a strange beginning for a reflection on the Trinity. Many times on this Sunday we find ourselves confronted with difficulty in understanding the specialized language of "three in one"—"one in three"—and we usually go home unmoved—and, perhaps, more than a bit puzzled by this most wonder-filled mystery at the core of our Christian faith—instead of being drawn more into the heart of God and being moved to live more fully—more deeply—to dance!

On this Sunday, we are invited to tap into the dynamic faith energy of the early followers of Jesus who experienced their life in God in a very personal way. Saint Paul states this well in his letter to the early Christian communities: "The grace of our Lord Jesus Christ, the love of God and the communion of the Holy Spirit be with all of you" (2 Cor 13:13). Grace, love, communion—"three" words that say something about the God who is around us, beside us, and within us. The challenge is to live our lives within this "three-ness" in such a way that makes a difference in our world so in need of grace, love, and communion. But, how can we do this?

When the early Greek Fathers of the Church spoke of this "three-ness,"they expressed it in terms of a dance and they used a very interesting term: *perichoresis*. This term isn't important but what it images is very important—it images the Trinity as a divine dance. Now, this dance is not for "two," where the two can be closed in upon themselves. It is rather a dance for "three" or more—a dance in a circle that moves to certain rhythms, in unpredictable ways and with lots of different steps. It is a dance into which everyone is invited.

And is this not what the Trinity is all about? God inviting us—each one of us—all of us—into a dance—into relationship—to be together with God, with one another, with all creation. The dance expands our boundaries, and to dance with God takes us into uncharted waters—to people we may not know and to places where we might not ordinarily go.

That sounds very nice, but what do we have to do—what do we have to learn—to dance with God and one another? Well, let's go back to Susan Sarandon: "I don't know how to dance; I don't know the steps." Who will teach us what the steps look like? Today's gospel tells us—the steps look like LOVE!

The Gospel from John makes this very clear: "God so loved the world and sent the Son. . . ." That means that God's love is prior to anything in our life. It is before all else. To continue the image of dance, we can say that God dances Jesus into the world because of this love and Jesus shares the music of this dance with all he meets so that ". . . whoever believes has eternal life."

But what does that really mean? I suggest that to believe is to have the courage to come close enough to hear God's invitation to life, to respond to the invitation and to learn the steps of the dance with one another—and I would like to reflect on three women in John's Gospel who had that courage. They are grace-filled models for us at each juncture of our lives.

The Samaritan woman, whom we meet in the fourth chapter of John, is quite courageous. She engages in conversation with Jesus—who is not only a stranger but also a Jew— and they have some startling exchanges—a dance, if you will, of steps back and forth as they discuss theological matters. This woman is bright and gutsy! She knows her "stuff." She knows her people, their history, and how they worship. At the same time, she is fascinated by Jesus and remains open to the conversation they are having. Her realization of who Jesus is causes her to run to bring her community into an ever-widening circle!

The scene is quite different in John 11, where we see Martha and Mary in their heartbreaking sorrow at the death of Lazarus. Perhaps with them, we ask: How can I dance when my heart is breaking? It took courage for them to say, "If you had been here my brother would not have died." And John's Gospel is clear: Jesus wept. From our life experiences, we know that not all dance is a "happy dance." As a person struggling for belief, how can I feel in my being that God is beside me in the darkness? Perhaps the courageous "dance step" here is one of letting my guard down to experience that when I am with others comfort can step in. Mary, Martha, Jesus—they are "three" in a circle of grief and then "four" in a circle of life restored. At this time in your life, do you want— do you need to be drawn into their circle?

And finally, John 20 brings us a glorious, heartfelt story—that of the meeting of Jesus and Mary of Magdala after the resurrection. Artist renditions of their meeting usually show Jesus standing and Mary clinging to his feet so that he says: "Do not continue to cling to me." But perhaps their meeting was not so static—perhaps, at the sound of her name, there was fire in her heart. Mary leaped for joy—and they began to dance!! And what courage Mary needed to "let go" and let Jesus dance into eternity while she danced to tell the rest: "I have seen the Lord!"

What is the story of your belief—of your courage—of your experience of the love of God that surrounds you, is beside you, and that, deep within, sets your heart on fire? The question before us on this Trinity Sunday is: Do we want to be a "one" alone? Or, do we want to learn the steps of love from one another, from all of creation, and from the Holy One?

Today we are invited to have our lives and relationships be a mirror of God's life—that of an ever widening circle of grace inviting us to join in the love of God for all.

So, shall we dance?

Solemnity of the
Body and Blood of Christ
A call to relationship

SUSAN HAARMAN

Deuteronomy 8:2–3, 14b–16a
Psalm 147:12–13, 14–15, 19–20
1 Corinthians 10:16–17
John 6:51–58

Right now, as I'm recording this video, the city of Chicago has been in shelter in place due to the COVID-19 outbreak for just under two months. Faced with a rapid change in my daily life and routine, my partner and I decided to deal with that as so many others have—by taking on a fairly ambitious baking project. We decided to try to make our own sourdough starter.

It failed. Spectacularly. Three different times.

As I watched our source of flour slowly begin to diminish, knowing that it was a very hot commodity and hard to find, I finally decided to phone a friend and try to figure out exactly where we were going wrong. I was being peppered with questions like, "Were you measuring the sourdough starter's temperature?" "Were you making sure to feed it at exactly the same time?" "Are you making sure to find an ideal spot that is not too warm, but not too cold?"

I just started thinking—*I was not aware that I was in an in-depth personal relationship with a baked good.*

Bread of Life Sunday looks really different during a global pandemic that limits so many people's ability to receive the Eucharist. For many of us, Holy Week and Easter Sunday came and went without our being able to take part in the core liturgical act—the reception of the Body and Blood of Christ. Without the Eucharist, how do we talk about what it means when Christ says, "I am the Bread of Life"?

As I read the first reading today and heard that reminder and admonition that "man does not live by bread alone, but on every word that comes from the mouth of God," I tried to take some comfort in it. But I just kept thinking: it's just not the same. Then I remembered, at the end of the day, that Eucharist begins and ends in a relationship. That's where it all comes from and where it all returns to.

I think it might be helpful for us to really engage this week's gospel reading if we have a sense of the context. Just before Jesus begins to explain to us what it means to be the living Bread of Life come down from heaven, he's actually just fed five thousand people. After this miracle, he heads off to pray, and when he comes back, the crowd is waiting for him and specifically tries to ask him where he's been and what's going on. Jesus fairly astutely wonders if they are there because they believe in him or because they want another meal. The group hedges their bets and says, "Well you know, Moses was able to produce bread in the desert, so maybe that's a sign you can give us that will help us believe in you." Christ responds saying "I am the bread of life"—I am what has come here to nourish you. A very long conversation follows, with the crowd continuing to ask for actual bread and Christ repeatedly saying, "I am the bread of life. I am the living bread." It's that recurrent admonition, that it is a relationship with Christ that people needed to be fed by, that's at the root of the Eucharist. It's a reminder of where the Eucharist comes from.

So it's that reminder of essential relationality of the Eucharist that I've been trying to re-engage with and remind myself of. I'm thankful in these moments to have what Andrew Greeley would call the "Catholic imagination." It's the sort of window that many of us tend to have where we can see God's movement and participation in all of life around us. God isn't this distant thing that we need to go out and find. Rather, God is invested and incarnated in the midst of our own lives, inviting us continually to feel God's presence and to feel God's love. It's in these *sacramental* moments, these moments that point back to the ways that we experience grace through the sacrament, that I find myself being fed and being reminded of what the reality of the Eucharist looks like for me.

I'm sure you can think of such moments as well. Maybe it was the first date or meeting that you had with a special person in your life across a cup of coffee or a glass of wine where you just found yourself grateful to be in their presence. Maybe it's during meals at family dinners where you've felt seen and loved. They are a subtle echo of the reality of the sacrament—Eucharist reminding us again to be *in relationship*. It's Christ over and over again reminding us "I am the living bread."

But it goes beyond just remembering. Relationships are about more than just what we receive. I think the words from the First Letter to the Corinthians are a great reminder that the Eucharist isn't a spectator sport. We *participate* in the body of Christ when we break the bread. We *participate* in the blood of Christ when we drink from the cup. Living into a eucharistic reality means participating in it. It means saying "yes" to that relationship again and again and again. It means trying to model the eucharistic relationship that God offers us to everyone around us.

That the Eucharist calls us to be in relationship is a challenge over and over again for us as believers and perhaps more importantly to us as a Church. At this time when we find ourselves so distant on this Bread of Life Sunday, how do we think about what it means to participate? To go beyond the boundaries of our own understanding of who fits and who doesn't? The Church in the United States still has not fully grappled with its participation in structural racism. The Church in the United States continues to advocate for the erosion of the rights and dignity of LGBTQ identified individuals. In direct opposition to the example Christ set. In direct opposition to the gospel. In flagrant, insidious, pernicious, and abusive opposition to the grace of the Eucharist.

I want to leave you with one final story. Years ago, I spent Easter Sunday in Kingston, Jamaica, at a place where children who had essentially been abandoned to die in a dump were able to live out their lives with dignity. In the middle of the Mass, a developmentally disabled child who had been making noises throughout most of the Mass stood up at the very moment of epiclesis. As the priest raised the host above his head, the child stood up, pointed, and shouted, "Jesus, Jesus, Jesus." Then he pointed to himself and said, "Jesus, Jesus, Jesus." And finally he pointed at the entire crowd and said, "Jesus, Jesus, Jesus." In that moment I knew that I had been fed far more than I could have ever imagined. So friends, as Christ reminds us that he's the living bread come down from heaven, how can we participate in that reality here and now?

Feast of Saint Mary of Magdala

Commissioned to speak

NONTANDO HADEBE

2 Corinthians 5:14–17
Psalm 63:2, 3–4, 5–6, 8–9
John 20:1–2, 11–18

I have chosen to do my reflection in a garden, because the garden plays a very significant place and role in the life of Mary Magdalene and in Christianity as a whole. Mary Magdalene, in the garden, we are told in the gospels, encountered the risen Christ. This was the first time that we heard the words of Mary Magdalene; it was the first time that she spoke in the gospels. And she spoke in the presence of Christ. Christ commissioned her to go and tell the disciples about the message of the resurrection. Now, the message of the resurrection is central to Christian faith. The apostle Paul tells us in 1 Corinthians 15 that without the resurrection of Christ there would be no Christianity. And so here we have a situation where Jesus entrusts to Mary Magdalene the very foundation of Christian faith: to go out and proclaim it, to speak, to open her mouth and speak to the apostles as an equal.

So who is Mary Magdalene in the life of Jesus? We see that Mary Magdalene was with Jesus in all the critical moments of his life. Luke 8:1–4 tells us that women were present in the company of the disciples with Jesus as they traveled around proclaiming the good news. We are told the names of women and Mary Magdalene is one of them. They were the ones who supported the ministry of Jesus, which means that Mary Magdalene was exposed to the teachings of Jesus. And then we see Mary Magdalene accompany Jesus to the cross. She and other women were there when the disciples were not there. The women were at the cross beside Jesus, listening to him, present with him in solidarity with his fate. And again in the resurrection narrative, it was Mary Magdalene who saw Jesus, the resurrected Jesus, for the first time. She was the first witness, and that's amazing! And Jesus said to her, "Go out." The risen Christ said, "You go out and proclaim," and gave her the apostolic commission to preach.

I want to go back to the garden, and this time it's the Garden of Eden. There we see Adam and Eve—that's where they were placed by God, and that's where sin entered. But I want to pick up on that narrative and what Saint Paul does with it in his letters. In Romans 5, Saint Paul describes Jesus as the second Adam. He says that sin came into the world through the first Adam, and Jesus is the second Adam through which grace and salvation comes to the world. But let's look at what he does with Eve. We go to 1 Timothy 2:12 where he says, "Women, be silent." Very interesting. Jesus says to Mary Magdalene, "Mary Magdalene, speak;" Saint Paul says, "Women, be silent." Because Eve was the one who was deceived, therefore Paul says, "I do not permit women to speak, I do not permit women to teach, I do not permit women to have authority over men." But in the garden when Mary Magdalene was with Jesus, Jesus said to Mary Magdalene, "Go and speak my word to the disciples," who were men.

So when we look at the apostolic tradition, we know that the apostolic tradition places itself with the Apostle Peter. He was the one given authority. So we, as women, trace our apostolic tradition to speak, to preach, and to have authority to Mary Magdalene, because that is what was given to her in the garden. Out of the mouth of Jesus, she was commissioned to speak. And so what we see in the life of Mary Magdalene we also see in the life of Christ: she was commissioned to speak, and then she was silenced by history. She was vilified. In other words, she was crucified. She was turned into a sex worker or a prostitute so that her witness would be silenced. And now we have a feast day; we are told that she's the apostle to the apostles. Very good.

So what are we going to do with that? We are going to trace our calling to preach, to speak, and to have authority to our apostle Mary Magdalene. She is going to establish a tradition for women, so that we, too, participate in the building of the Church. Mary Magdalene was given authority directly by Jesus to speak, to proclaim, to have power. So in celebrating this feast day, we affirm Mary Magdalene as apostle to the apostles, and we trace our ministry as women to her apostleship. And so we enter into a new era, where women preach, where women speak. Not only do we preach and speak and witness to the gospel, but we speak for ourselves. We regain our voices, we speak of what it means to be a woman in a patriarchy: silenced, vilified, crucified, told that you stay there, you don't speak. We speak our stories, we speak our vision, we speak our thoughts, we speak our mind, we enter every sphere of society as speaking, empowered, powerful women. We enter into the sphere of our Church under the commission of Jesus following the apostolic tradition of Mary Magdalene, commissioned to speak, commissioned to go, commissioned for activity. The silencing of women does not get its support from Jesus. We get our support to speak from Jesus. That's why Catholic women preach, Catholic women speak.

Today as we celebrate the apostolic tradition of Mary Magdalene, we rise up as women. And we say we have a tradition that can be traced to Jesus, that can be traced to a direct command from Jesus to speak. To speak. And we shall speak, we shall speak with authority, we shall speak with intelligence, and we shall speak for ourselves. And we will create a parallel tradition that empowers women. We live in a world where women are violated. They are violated. Why? Because they are violatable. We live in a world where women are abused. Why? Because they've been abusable. We live in a world where women are excluded. Why? Because they are excludable. We are saying through the apostolic tradition of Mary Magdalene that this stops. We are going to rise up as empowered women, knowing that Christ stands with us to speak, to no longer be the subjects of vilification, no longer be the subjects of abuse and violence. We are going to rise up. Jesus rose; he was violated, but he rose in a body that can no longer be violated. So when we proclaim resurrection, we look forward to a resurrected body that no longer is violated, and that is the apostolic commission, the apostolic tradition for women through Mary Magdalene.

We celebrate Mary Magdalene as women. So we pray: *We consult you, our apostle, the one who directly saw and lived and walked with Jesus. Just as you witness his resurrected body beyond violation, help us to have bodies beyond violation, voices beyond violation, so that we, too, can speak, can be empowered, and can rise in your apostolic tradition. We pray. Amen.*

Feast of the Transfiguration

A feast of visionary hope

MARY ROSE D'ANGELO

Daniel 7:9–10, 13–14
Psalm 97:1–2, 5–6, 9
2 Peter 1:16–19
Matthew 17:1–9

Today's reading from 2 Peter evokes the voice of the long dead apostle. Recalling first the glorious mountain vision, the heavenly voice, he goes on to remind the readers: "We have more firmly the prophetic word, to which you do well to attend, as to a lamp shining in a dark place, until the day dawns and the daystar rises in your hearts" (2 Pet 1:19).

The feast of the Transfiguration is a feast of visionary hope, a glimpse of what is not yet, showing itself as already present. The splendor revealed to the three apostles on the mountain is the beginning of multiple fulfillments and promises. Immediately before the transfiguration in the gospel, Jesus makes a promise that at first reading seems unfulfilled. To hearers stunned by the passion prediction and warnings of the cost of discipleship (Matt 16:21–27), Jesus promises that some of them will live to see "the Son of Man coming in his kingdom" (16:28). Yet some see exactly that, and at once: these three, awed, confused, and silenced as they are. What they see is a foretaste of the resurrection, when silence will be replaced by the proclamation that "the Son of Man is risen from the dead" (Matt 17:9) through the visions and testimony of the witnesses: first the two Marys, then the eleven, then all readers and all hearers of the gospel, "until the completion of the age" (Matt 28:9–10, 16–20).

And Jesus's resurrection itself is a beginning, the "first fruits of those who have fallen asleep" (1 Cor 15:20). The feast of the Transfiguration, like the feast of the Assumption, celebrates the promise of human solidarity in transformation: what has happened to Jesus will happen also to us. The feast of the Transfiguration speaks to me most strongly of this hope, for this day was the earthly birthday of my late friend and theological colleague Catherine Mowry LaCugna. This feast, then, is a beacon guiding us from and to the vision of God's glory that we have glimpsed in living human beings (cf. Irenaeus, *Adv Haer* 4.20.7), toward a communion of saints now as the daystar rises in our hearts and finally in the fullness of day.

But the transfiguration offers visions of hope also for our eschatological present, the time between the resurrection of Jesus and the transformation of the world. Its key is the recognition that the "Son of Man" of the gospels is also the "Son of Man," the human figure, of Daniel's dream. Daniel's vision comes from a very dark place; it begins as a nightmare of monsters, beasts of hybrid parts embodying the confusion and horror of the successive empires of the ancient world: their wars of conquest, their exploitation of colonies, their projects of cultural dominance that had formed the world the Jews of the second century BCE endured (Dan 7:1–8, 15–25). Like the beasts, the "one like a son of man" is not just a ruler, but a reign, an empire: the one like a son of man, the reign of God and of the saints. Daniel envisions the monstrous empires falling away before a reign with a human face (7:9–14, 26–27).

Jesus and the women and men who were his companions in the reign of God movement lived under yet another plundering empire, another regime under which untold numbers of Jewish women and men were crucified, enslaved, excluded from political rights, exiled, targeted by xenophobia, subjected to violence and abuse so some few could prosper. In this context, Jesus and his companions preached a reign in which the hungry are fed, the sick healed, the afflicted comforted, the prisoners set free, and there is constant good news for the poor, news of freedom, justice, and mercy for all. Like many others, Jesus died at the hands of Rome, condemned in the Roman imperial self-interest.

Ours is another dark time, when work toward justice and mercy is under threat, and efforts for the relief and consolation of refugees, migrants, the sick and the disabled, the aging and the frail; the very young, women and children lacking prenatal care, women and children threatened by famine and war; men, women and children imprisoned unjustly or long beyond justice: all, all are under direct assault. The victory and reign of the human figure of Daniel, the "son of man" of Matthew, seem very far away. Yet the vision of God's reign is a reminder that God's great good news is for the multitudes in this world as well as the next. The transfiguration pushes us to hope and commitment: the lamp of our saints and heroes, of the prophetic word, of the dawning vision shining in a dark place, pulling us forward until the day breaks and the daystar rises in our hearts.

Solemnity of the Assumption

Not tethered to the Earth

Joan Chittister, OSB

Revelation 11:19a; 12:1–6a, 10ab
Psalm 45:10, 11, 12, 16
1 Corinthians 15:20–27
Luke 1:39–56

Good morning everybody—Happy Feast Day!

It's the Assumption of Mary into heaven, and the question is, what can that feast and its historical meanings possibly have to say to us today?

Well, first of all, the feast of the Assumption is clearly the feast of Mary's total identity with the mind and heart of God.

But, what does it have to say to us? With our lives and our struggles, with our erratic attempts to give ourselves totally to God while the world around us—and never forget, the world within us, too—are clamoring ceaselessly for our attention? And if truth were known, they want our commitment as well.

The fact is that life can be a very sticky thing: there are some things that simply cannot be escaped. For instance, remember that feeling of failure that can cling to a person for years, maybe; or possibly that great sense of loss that weighed our hearts to the ground, perhaps; or the notion that what we have been striving for all our lives and will never be able to claim as we had hoped, slipped our grasp.

Oh, indeed, life is not what we expected it to be in the here and now. In fact, life is not what we want it to be—ever.

So where do we go when people make light of our dashed desires and say to us, "Would you just forget it! You'll get over it. . . . Time cures everything."

Really? Well, maybe it does, if by "cure" you mean that all of life simply goes dull now. The sharp pain of disappointment has ended, that's true, but nothing good, it seems, has come to replace it.

So, we reconcile ourselves to life in the slow lane—after all, there's nothing to rush to now, is there?

There's nothing left to hope for and what was once our faith in the god of good times has gone dry.

So what are we to do, except maybe stop trying so hard. But then when we do that, we lose our sense of purpose or we simply go through the motions maybe, but down deep the cavern of disappointment still lingers, still darkens our souls, still depresses our spirit mightily. It takes the joy out of the very footprints and footsteps of life.

It's then, however, that two images call us beyond ourselves: First the song of the psalmist.

Oh sure, long forgotten, maybe, but listen carefully, because at these moments the words of that psalm are crying out to us again.

Just when we feel that things can't get much worse, Psalm 16 sings in the far reaches of our dulled souls: "You will not allow the one you love to see the pit; you will reveal the path of life to me."

Indeed, the message is clear, isn't it? Those whom God loves—the psalm promises and Mary of Nazareth was raised to know—will be raised up above the thousand daily deaths that come into every life.

When we refuse to become imprisoned by things and status and ambition and self and greed—the greed of a whole society that considers things the be-all and end-all of life—our souls are set free and our bodies are unburdened to rise with our hearts to live again.

Then life becomes truly livable. Enough becomes enough. God becomes God again. It is all a matter, you see, of learning to let go, of letting go of what it is that chains us to earth.

What model is there for us of the possibility? What proof do we have that we too can rise above the fleeting things we want, to become what we are fully, wholly meant to be? What hope do we have that however much we've lost before—and may in fact be losing now, at this moment—there is much more yet to be gained of the good and the true and the really beautiful in life? Where can we go to find someone whose life is not tethered to the earth to the point of death?

It's to Mary, the model of all our losses in life;

It's to Mary, the mother of hope in the midst of despair;

It's to Mary, the woman of courage, who sees everything in her life lost and yet, at the same time, her eternal faith reaches out and lifts her up to find the higher, the richer, the more meaningful things of life, as she did, both here and hereafter.

The answer to the kind of depression that comes with loss and failure, with being chained to the things of earth, surely is Mary of the Assumption whose love of God lifted her heart far above the loves and goals and gains of those who had never really seen the Christ for what he was because their mind's eye was taken up totally with what they were themselves.

Life can become, you see, all about me.

And this is exactly when the feast of the Assumption takes on the meaning that our childhood spiritual imaginations could never summon, could never have seen.

Mary of the Assumption teaches us to keep our eyes on the things of heaven, to free ourselves from the fetters of anything less, to develop a vision larger than ourselves and outside of ourselves, and to allow ourselves to be lifted up beyond the petty and the transient to the eternal and the unalloyed.

Mary of the Assumption is a sign of what we can also become, if we are willing to let go of what we have planned for ourselves and lift our hearts to higher things.

The prayer at the heart of this great feast, of total immersion in the mind and will and heart of God, is: "Mary, woman of freedom, be with me, be with all of us—as we struggle with whatever it is that is holding us down again."

Happy Feast Day, Happy Assumption in your own life forever.

Solemnity of All Saints

The path of the beatitudes

MARGUERITE BARANKITSE

Revelation 7:2–4, 9–14
Psalm 24:1bc–2, 3–4ab, 2–6
1 John 3:1–3
Matthew 5:1–12a

On this Solemnity of All Saints, I would like to begin my remarks in the style of Isaiah 60:1–5.

> Stand! Shine! For here is the light, and over you rises the Glory of the Lord! Look around and see that all are gathered, they come to you. Your sons come from far away and your daughters are carried in their arms. Then you will see and be radiant! Your heart will tremble and expand!!!

Yes, All Saints' Day is a message of immense hope! The Gospel of Saint Matthew today invites us to happiness—a happiness beyond all names! "Blessed, Blessed!" Eight times, our Lord repeats it to his disciples as a hymn to happiness!

In proclaiming this incredible message, dazzling even in its demands, such as, "Blessed are those who weep," or "Blessed are those who are persecuted for justice," Jesus sends us his image. He is the man of the beatitudes. Only he fully lived them. He is our master in holiness, our model and our path.

In baptism, we were immersed in his Easter mystery of death and resurrection. "All the elect must go through this great ordeal, wash their clothes in the Blood of the Lamb" (Rev 7:17).

The path of the beatitudes is indeed often rough! But the Risen One leads us there in his wake. He holds us firmly, to lead us where we might not have wanted to go ourselves.

May his strength therefore sustain our life and make the desire for holiness, for which we are made, grow in us!

It is a holiness not to be won by our own strength but to receive from our Father, by his Son, as the most beautiful gift.

Yes, a sublime gift that we will, in our turn, distribute.

Contemplating the Solemnity of All Saints urges us to marvel at God's vision for humanity, at the diversity of the gifts of the Holy Spirit, and at the ways in which each and every one of us responds.

Today we also celebrate the saints of our respective countries, those who fell under the machetes of genocide in our two countries where I was born, Burundi and Rwanda. Yes, the saints of our families, those who died because of fratricidal hatred. The saints in the streets who die to save others. Those in prison. Those who fall ill in hospitals, like the chaplains in Italy: sixty priests who died of COVID-19 to save the forgotten in elderly care homes, in refugee camps. The saints who drowned to save others in the Mediterranean, those who tried to cross borders to give their children better lives.

Yes, as Father Daniel Ange said, this feast reveals to us once and for all that our world is a wellspring of untapped holiness.

Would that we could be bold enough to proclaim it, in our turn, throughout "the excruciatingly malnourished deserts of our world, deprived of the most basic foods, deprived of breast milk."

Yes, let us walk with confidence in the path of Christ, supported by prayer and the example of the saints, those the liturgy presents to us and those we encounter as we move through our days.

Let us move forward joyfully, until the day when we can finally fully taste the fruits of life.

Yes, this is our Blessed Hope.

Solemnity of Christ the King

Jesus, hidden in plain sight

NORMA PIMENTEL, MJ

Ezekiel 34:11–12, 15–17
Psalm 23:1–2, 2–3, 5–6
1 Corinthians 15:20–26, 28
Matthew 25:31–46

I would like to begin by sharing with you a video I saw recently about a blind man who is sitting near the steps in front of a building with a sign that says, "I'M BLIND, PLEASE HELP." People pass by and don't seem to notice him. They just walk on by as they continue on their route. One morning a woman passes by and then returns. She looks at the man, picks up the sign, and writes a message on the other side.

Amazingly, after she walks away almost everybody stops and gives this man some coins, some money. On her way back, perhaps after work, the woman stops and looks at the man. He senses that it is the person who wrote on his sign that morning. He asks her, "What did you write on my sign?" And she says, "I wrote the same thing, but with different words." What she wrote was, "IT'S A BEAUTIFUL DAY AND I CAN'T SEE IT."

It's amazing how our attitude, our response changes when we see people with different eyes. Just like this blind man, there are many others in our world, in our society, in our community who really don't have the opportunity to truly experience the beauty of life. The Solemnity of Christ the King invites us to bring Jesus into our lives, to live out our faith. How can we do this? By responding to the Lord Jesus's invitation to find him in the people who we see who need our help. We find him in the blind man and also in the immigrant or the poor, people who are in distress. We are invited on this day and every day to live out our faith, to make a difference in the lives of others.

Here in South Texas, we respond to a reality we see every day with the immigrants who arrive at the U.S.-Mexico border. We try to help them. We try to restore their dignity so that they can become people who are appreciated, who know that they are children of God and that God loves them. The work is done by many people who opt to make a difference in the lives of those in need. These are generous and loving people who choose to live out their faith and to make a difference by welcoming and embracing the fathers, mothers, and children who arrive tired and hungry.

The Lord invites us to not be indifferent to suffering, but instead to make that suffering part of who we are by welcoming people and making a difference by reaching out and caring for them. The greatest gift that we have is the gift of love that God gives us so abundantly. What is the point of receiving that love if we don't share it? We must share it with others. We must share it especially with those who need us. This is what Jesus is inviting us to and wants us to do—to really be there for those who need us, those who are marginalized, those who are out there who are ignored by many in our society. Those who some think we can just discard. The Solemnity of Christ the King presents us with an opportunity to really look at our faith and begin to question: "What am I doing?" "What can I do?" As followers of Jesus Christ, the most urgent priority that we have is to see the face of Jesus in every human being, especially those who are most vulnerable in our community. Jesus invites us to encounter him. We're not going to find Jesus on the cross; we're going to find him among us, in plain sight. He even showed us and told us how to look. He said, "You will find me. I was hungry and you gave me food. I was thirsty and you gave me something to drink. I was a stranger and you welcomed me. I was in prison, and you visited me."

What happens sometimes is that we are afraid. We are afraid to come out of ourselves, out of our comfort zones. It takes only that first step, that first step that will help us encounter Jesus. It becomes easier after that. It is there that we find salvation. It is there that we find the kingdom of God.

Preacher Biographies

Louise Akers, SC (deceased)

Sister of Charity Louise Akers, DMin, was known for her tireless work for justice within the Church and in the world. Her ministries included justice education and advocacy in formal classroom settings at both the high school and university levels; parish coordinator in the Archdiocesan Social Action Office of Cincinnati; founder and coordinator of Cincinnati's Intercommunity Justice and Peace Center; social concerns director of the Leadership Conference of Women Religious (LCWR); and coordinator of the Sisters of Charity Office of Peace, Justice and Integrity of Creation. She earned a master's degree in theology (1974) and completed her doctor of ministry degree with a project entitled "Patriarchal Power and the Pauperization of Women."

Anne Arabome, SSS

Sr. Anne Arabome is a member of the Sisters of Social Service in Los Angeles. She is currently the associate director of the Faber Center for Ignatian Spirituality at Marquette University in Milwaukee. Sr. Anne holds a doctor of ministry (DMin) degree in spirituality from Catholic Theological Union in Chicago, and a PhD in systematic theology from the University of Roehampton in London, UK. She is the co-founder (in 2015) of Wellspring Africa, a program that supports HIV/AIDS orphan girls in Kibera slum in Nairobi, Kenya, and co-founder (in 2021) of the Daughters of St. Josephine Bakhita Project—an interfaith initiative to transform the lives of vulnerable girls and young women in The Gambia through training programs, entrepreneurial skills, and dignifying employment. She is the author of *Why Do You Trouble This Woman? Women and the Spiritual Exercises of St. Ignatius of Loyola* (Paulist Press, 2022).

Sister Anita P. Baird, DHM

Sister Anita Baird, a member of the Religious Congregation of the Society of the Daughters of the Heart of Mary, has served as regional superior, provincial councilor, and United States provincial. A native of Chicago, she earned a bachelor of arts (BA) degree in sociology from DePaul University and a master of arts (MA) degree in theological studies from Loyola University Chicago, and in 2013 she was awarded an honorary DMin degree from Catholic Theological Union. In 1997, she became the first African American to serve as chief of staff to the archbishop of Chicago, Cardinal Francis George, who in 2000 appointed her the founding director of the Archdiocesan Office for Racial Justice. A past president of the National Black Sisters' Conference, she received the organization's Harriet Tubman "Moses of Her People" Award. In 2018 she received the Outstanding Leadership Award from the Leadership Conference of Women Religious.

Marguerite Barankitse

Marguerite Barankitse, better known as "Maggy," was born in Ruyigi, Burundi, in 1956. After studying to become a teacher, she pursued three years of theological studies in Lourdes, France, before returning to Ruyigi to teach French in a secondary school. There, at the age of twenty-three, Maggy adopted one of her orphaned students, the first of five she would welcome into her home. In 1993 ethnic violence erupted in Burundi. Maggy, who was working as secretary to the bishop in Ruyigi, witnessed powerlessly the massacre of seventy-two people, but managed to convince the killers to spare twenty-five children. As the chaos continued, she took in more orphans without distinction. Her mission would be to fight against hatred and indifference, giving to her children, and to the forty-seven thousand who would follow them, an alternative, a home of peace and love: "Maison Shalom." She has received many recognitions and awards, and continues to advocate for Burundian refugees.

Terry Battaglia

Terry Battaglia was born and raised in Ohio in an Italian Catholic family. She knew at a very young age that she wanted to minister in the Church. She has been in full-time ministry for the past forty-one years. Terry and her husband Bob Mlakar have been married for more than thirty-one years. Their family is growing; their daughter Nickie, son David and his wife Alicia, and daughter Josephina all live in Valley View, Ohio. Terry currently is a pastoral minister at Church of the Resurrection in Solon, Ohio.

Dianne Bergant, CSA

Dianne Bergant, CSA, is Carroll Stuhlmueller, CP Distinguished Professor Emerita of Old Testament Studies at Catholic Theological Union in Chicago. She served as president of the Catholic Biblical Association of America (2000–2001). For more than twenty-five years she has been Old Testament book reviewer for *The Bible Today*, and for five years served as the magazine's general editor. Her weekly column, "The Word," for *America* magazine (2002–2005) was later published as a book by Paulist Press. She is currently working in the areas of biblical interpretation and biblical theology, particularly in relation to issues of peace, ecology and feminism. Her many books include: *People of the Covenant: An Invitation to the Old Testament*; *Song of Songs* (Berit Olam Series), *Lamentations* (Abingdon Old Testament Commentaries); *Living the Word: Scripture Reflections and Commentaries for Sundays and Holy Days*; *Rejoice in God's Reign: Daily Advent Reflection and Prayer*; *Genesis: In the Beginning*; and *A New Heaven, A New Earth*.

Rachel Bundang

Dr. Rachel Bundang is a Catholic feminist ethicist presently based in the Bay Area. She teaches as a member of the religious studies faculty at Sacred Heart Prep in Atherton and in the Graduate Program for Pastoral Ministries at Santa Clara University. She has written multiple articles and book chapters and has served on the editorial team for the journal *Theological Studies*. A founding member of the Asian Pacific American Religious Research Initiative (APARRI), her areas of interest lie at the intersections of race, feminisms, technology, inequality, and Catholic social teaching. As a liturgist, she preaches and leads music regularly at her home parish in the Bay Area and also offers retreats and workshops nationally.

Christine Elisabeth Burke, IBVM

Christine Burke, IBVM (Loreto), who lives in Quezon City, Philippines, was engaged for many years in adult faith education in the archdiocese of Adelaide, Australia. Her PhD dissertation dealt with how the Christian tradition could speak more relevantly to a secular society. In the 1990s, Christine pioneered the Church Ministry Program at Catholic Theological College in Adelaide, which helps form lay pastoral leaders for parishes. As a feminist theologian, Christine is interested in ways of helping people connect daily life with the gospel and explore new possibilities for our Church. After serving from 2005 to 2011 as province leader for the IBVM sisters in Australia, Vietnam, and East Timor, Christine moved to the Philippines in late 2013 to begin a House of Studies for younger sisters from the province. Christine's books include: *Freedom Justice and Sincerity: Reflections on the Life and Spirituality of Mary Ward* as well as *Through a Woman's Eyes,* which presents meditations on and feminist insights into gospel stories.

Simone Campbell, SSS

Sister Simone Campbell (a Roman Catholic Sister of Social Service) is a religious leader, attorney, and author with extensive experience in public policy and advocacy for systemic change. For almost seventeen years she was the executive director of NET-WORK Lobby for Catholic Social Justice, and leader of Nuns on the Bus. In 2010, she wrote the "nuns' letter" that was influential in the passage of the Affordable Care Act. She has twice spoken at Democratic National Conventions and has received many awards. Prior to her work in Washington, she did interfaith state-based advocacy in Sacramento and for eighteen years was the founder and lead attorney at the Community Law Center in Oakland. Her two books, *A Nun on the Bus* (2014) and *Hunger for Hope* (2020), are award-winning reflections on the substance of her life and the call to faithful justice seeking.

Francine Cardman (deceased)

Francine Cardman, who died in 2021, was associate professor of historical theology and church history at Boston College School of Theology and Ministry. She wrote and lectured on early Christian ethics and spirituality, ministry and leadership in the early Church, and questions of gender and justice in contemporary church practice. Her many publications included essays on Augustine, women's ministries and ordination in early Christianity, structures of governance and accountability in the Church past and present, the development of early Christian ethics, and Vatican II and ecumenism. A past president of the North American Academy of Ecumenists, she served on the Eastern Orthodox/Roman Catholic Consultation of the USCCB and was a board member and vice-president of NETWORK. In 2021, she was honored for her lifetime achievement in a day-long symposium on "The Role of Women in Theological Education: Celebrating the Contributions of Professor Francine Cardman."

Krista Chinchilla-Patzke

Krista Chinchilla-Patzke serves as a university minister for Ministry en lo Cotidiano at Dominican University in River Forest, Illinois. Previously, she served as the campus minister for

Catholic Social Concerns and Service at Marian University in Indianapolis, Indiana, where she oversaw service and immersion opportunities for undergraduate students. She earned an MA in theology and ministry from the School of Theology and Ministry at Boston College and a BA in theology and psychology from Loyola Marymount University. Her Jesuit education has greatly influenced her passion for justice and her love for theology. Krista was born in Guatemala City, Guatemala, and raised in Southern California, two places that have significantly shaped her understanding of community. She is grateful for her partner and her family, who have taught her the importance of welcoming all to a table where bread is to be broken in unity.

Joan Chittister, OSB

A Benedictine Sister of Erie, PA, Sister Joan has served as president of the Leadership Conference of Women Religious (LCWR) and was prioress of her community for twelve years. The founder and executive director of Benetvision, a resource and research center for contemporary spirituality, she is also a founding member of The Global Peace Initiative of Women, a partner organization of the UN, which works to develop a worldwide network of women peace builders. Sister Joan is an international lecturer and award-winning author of sixty books. She has won sixteen Catholic Press Association awards, the *U.S. Catholic* magazine Award for Furthering the Cause of Women in the Church, as well as recognition for her work for justice, peace, and equality, especially for women, in church and in society. A regular online columnist for the *National Catholic Reporter*, she is one of the most articulate social analysts and influential religious leaders of this age.

Donna L. Ciangio, OP

Sr. Donna, a Dominican Sister of Caldwell, New Jersey, holds a doctorate from Drew University. She serves as the chancellor of the Archdiocese of Newark. Previously, she served as the director of Church Leadership Consultation, where she worked internationally and nationally in promoting parish vitality and pastoral direction, congregational and leadership development, faith formation, and many other areas. She has served as international coordinator for Renew, as director of pastoral services of the National Pastoral Life Center, and as parish consultant for the Jesuit Conference USA. Sister Donna also served as the director of adult faith formation at St. Rose of Lima Church in Short Hills, New Jersey, and as an adjunct professor in Drew University's doctor of ministry program. Among her many writings, she is the co-author of *Open Our Hearts: A Small Group Guide for an Active Lent* (Ave Maria Press).

Karen Clifton

Karen Clifton is the founding executive director of the Catholic Mobilizing Network (CMN). Her work against the death penalty began in 1996 in Houston, Texas, when her social justice and advocacy projects intersected with those of Sr. Helen Prejean, CSJ. This relationship resulted in the 2008 formation of CMN in partnership with the Congregation of St. Joseph Sisters. Karen holds an MDiv degree from University of St. Thomas, St. Mary's School of Theology. She is currently executive coordinator of the Catholic Prison Ministries Coalition (CPMC) which was formed in 2018. In 2011 she was awarded the 2011 Servitor Pacis Award by the Path to Peace Foundation of the Mission of the Vatican to the United Nations. Karen is the mother of five adult children and grandmother of ten grandchildren.

Jocelyn E. Collen

Jocelyn E. Collen has an MDiv from Boston College School of Theology and Ministry. She studied theology at Fairfield University as an undergraduate with Paul Lakeland and Nancy Dallavalle. She holds a post-master's Certificate in spiritual formation from Boston College. Jocelyn is the associate director of Life Together, the Episcopal Service Corps program in Boston. In the past she has served as religious educator, chaplain, faith formation assistant, and campus minister, and she is currently serving on a ministry team that presides over communion services at a prison in Boston, Massachusetts. She is an executive member of the FutureChurch board of trustees.

M. Shawn Copeland

M. Shawn Copeland is professor emerita of systematic theology in the Department of Theology of the Morrissey College and Graduate School of Arts and Sciences at Boston College. Copeland's research and writing focus on shifts in theological understanding of the human person; suffering, solidarity, and the cross of Jesus of Nazareth in probing conditions under which human persons may flourish authentically; and thematizing an African American Catholic theology. Her books include *Enfleshing Freedom: Body, Race, and Being*; *The Subversive Power of Love: The Vision of Henriette Delille*; and *Knowing Christ Crucified: The Witness of African American Religious Experience*. Professor Copeland is a former convener of the Black Catholic Theological Symposium (BCTS). She was the first African American to serve as president of the Catholic Theological Society of America (CTSA), from which, in 2018, she was also awarded the society's highest honor, the John Courtney Murray Award.

Emily Cortina

Emily is a married layperson with three young children who strives to live joyfully through her children's eyes. An active promoter of restorative justice in all facets of life, she currently serves as coordinator of outreach and formation with Kolbe House Jail Ministry of the Archdiocese of Chicago. In this role, Emily leads outreach to parishes and to families affected by incarceration, living out her vocational call to be an agent of structural change while fostering the personal relationships and encounters that fuel and sustain it. She was drawn into the world of criminal justice through her husband's incarceration experience as a Mexican immigrant, and she was further introduced to principles of restorative justice while accompanying youth in detention with Precious Blood Ministry of Reconciliation. She earned an MA in intercultural ministry from Catholic Theological Union and a BA in economics and journalism from Creighton University.

Kathy Lilla Cox

Kathy Lilla Cox is a research associate in the Department of Theology and Religious Studies at the University of San Diego. Her PhD in theology is from Fordham University. She taught theology for eleven years at the College of St. Benedict, St. John's University, and St. John's School of Theology and Seminary in central Minnesota. She is the author of *Water Shaping Stone: Faith, Relationships, and Conscience Formation* (Liturgical Press, 2015). Her current book project, tentatively titled *The Communal Nature of Conscience Formation: Journeying toward Justice,* focuses on how moral formation in communities contributes to both well-formed and malformed moral agents. This work considers anew the role of bodies, emotions, and affections in moral formation informed by recent biological and social science research. Ignatian and Benedictine spirituality, along with various individual and communal prayer practices, feed the labor of her theological research and her life.

Jane M. Cruthirds

Jane is a mother and lay ecclesial minister living in Louisville, Kentucky. Her joy is raising her son, Duncan. Jane's professional ministry focuses on developing a culture of evangelization and discipleship at St. Michael Catholic Church in Jeffersontown, Kentucky. She is also an active member of St. Michael's where her stewardship of time and talent is proclaiming the word of God, making a joyful noise with the adult choir, and helping adults in the parish to learn more about their faith. Jane is a veteran of the United States Air Force. She earned a master's degree in pastoral studies from Loyola University New Orleans, where she was honored with the Loyola Institute of Ministry Scholar Award.

Diana Culbertson, OP

Diana Culbertson, OP, of the Dominican Sisters of Peace is professor emerita at Kent State University, where she directed the undergraduate program in English, the program of Religious Studies, and the graduate program of Liberal Studies. She received her PhD in comparative literature from the University of North Carolina at Chapel Hill and her MA in theology from Aquinas Institute of Theology. She is the former president of the Colloquium on Violence and Religion and a board member of FutureChurch. Her published works include *The Poetics of Revelation: Recognition and the Narrative Tradition* (Mercer University Press); *Rose Hawthorne Lathrop: Selected Writings* (Paulist Press); *Invisible Light: Poems about God* (Columbia University Press). She is a former editor and writer for the Center for Learning and author of *God in a World of Violence, The Meaning of Faith, The Meaning of Hope, The Scandal of the Parables, The Body of Christ,* and *Life in the World to Come.*

Mary Rose D'Angelo

Mary R. D'Angelo is professor emerita at the University of Notre Dame. She lectures and writes on New Testament, Christian origins, and women's studies. Her areas of interest are women and gender in antiquity, ancient Jewish and Christian exegesis, and imperial politics as a context of ancient Jewish and Christian writings, as well as the contemporary use of scripture in liturgy and spirituality. She is the author of *Moses in the Letter to the Hebrews.* Her current projects include a feminist commentary on 1 Corinthians and a project investigating Roman imperial moral propaganda as a context for Jewish and Christian "family values." She served on the editorial board of the *Journal of Biblical Literature* for twelve years and on the board of the *Catholic Biblical Quarterly* for six years. She received a Mentoring Award from the Society of Biblical Literature Committee on the Status of Women in the Profession in 2005.

Petra Dankova

Petra Dankova is a researcher and lecturer at the University of Applied Sciences Würzburg–Schweinfurt (Germany) working at the intersection of mobility, migration, and transnational social work. Additionally, she has over ten years of work experience developing and leading projects for displaced and mobile people. She has worked extensively with both faith-based and secular organizations and focuses on the fields of mental health and psychosocial services, education, and rights-based community development. She holds a master's in social work (MSW) from Boston College and a BA in political science from the University of Notre Dame. Originally from the Czech Republic, she currently lives and works in Germany.

Joan S. Dawber, SC

Sister Joan Dawber, a member of the Sisters of Charity Halifax, was born in Manchester, England. After moving to the United States, she graduated from St. John's University with a BA in Human Services and an MA in Theology. She also holds a master's degree in pastoral studies from Loyola University, Chicago. After twenty years working as a pastoral associate in the Diocese of Brooklyn and Queens, New York, she began to work full time in an initiative to combat trafficking in persons. In 2007 she incorporated *LifeWay Network, Inc.*, working to create safe homes for victims of human trafficking in the New York area. She serves on the Sisters of Charity Global Concerns Resource Team, is the former co-chair of the New York Coalition of Religious Congregations—Stop Trafficking in Persons (NY-CRC-STOP), and is a former member of the board of the U.S. Catholic Sisters Against Human Trafficking (USCSAHT).

Marie Dennis

Marie Dennis is senior advisor to the secretary general of Pax Christi International. She was co-president of Pax Christi from

2007 to 2019 and serves on the executive committee of Pax Christi's Catholic Nonviolence Initiative. She was one of the primary organizers of the April 2016 conference on Nonviolence and Just Peace that was cosponsored by the Vatican and Pax Christi International. Marie was previously director of the Maryknoll Office for Global Concerns. She is a Secular Franciscan, author or co-author of seven books, including *Choosing Peace: The Catholic Church Returns to Gospel Nonviolence*. She holds a master's degree in moral theology from Washington Theological Union and honorary doctorates from Trinity Washington University and Alvernia University. She has previously served on the White House Task Force on Global Poverty and Development and on the national boards of JustFaith Ministries, *Sojourners* magazine, the Jubilee USA Network, and several other organizations.

Molleen Dupree-Dominguez

Molleen is a teacher, writer, and minister living in the beautiful Bay Area of northern California. She earned an MDiv from the Jesuit School of Theology at Santa Clara University in 2003, along with a Certificate in Spiritual Direction in 2004. At Bishop O'Dowd High School she teaches courses on Christian morality, ethics and media, spiritual ecology as well as other courses in religious studies. Her most recent podcast project, *On a Mission,* is on iTunes. She speaks and writes on the topic of getting real and going deep with God and is an experienced retreat facilitator and spiritual director. Molleen is married and has one daughter. Her online home is molleendupreedominguez.com.

Margaret A. Farley

Margaret Farley, a member of the Sisters of Mercy of the Americas, West Midwest Community, is Gilbert L. Stark Professor Emerita of Christian Ethics at Yale University Divinity School. She is the author or co-editor of eight books, including *Just Love: A Framework for Christian Sexual Ethics* (winner of the 2008

Grawemeyer Award), and *Changing the Questions: Explorations in Christian Ethics,* as well as more than two hundred articles and book chapters on various topics in ethics. She also holds fourteen honorary degrees. She was co-director of the All-Africa Conference: Sister to Sister, an organization that has facilitated the work of women in sub-Saharan Africa responding to the AIDS pandemic. She is past president of both the Society of Christian Ethics and the Catholic Theological Society of America, from which she received the John Courtney Murray Award for Excellence in Theology. She was a founding member of Yale–New Haven Hospital's Bioethics Committee.

Ruth Fehlker

Ruth Fehlker lives in Coesfeld, Germany. She holds a master's degree (*Diplom*) in Catholic theology from the University of Münster and a Certificate in Pastoral Psychology and a Certificate in Pastoral Theology which she earned after training with the Diocese of Münster for four years. She works as a pastoral worker (*Pastoralreferentin*) in the parish of St. Lamberti in Coesfeld. She is a member of the women's council to the bishop in the Diocese of Münster. She regularly leads liturgies of the word, preaches during Mass and also leads funerals. She is part of the team of pastoral workers who publish a "Thought for the Day" on local radio in a one-minute format. She has been part of the network Catholic Women Speak since 2015. Her spirituality is strongly influenced by the community of Taizé and its vision of a united church.

Jutta Battenberg Galindo

Jutta Battenberg Galindo has been professor of theology at the Universidad Iberoamericana (UIA) and at the Franciscan Institute of Philosophy and Theology (IFFT) of the Province of the Holy Gospel in Mexico City since 2006. She is also director of the Center for Human Development and Spirituality Domus Vitae, AC. She earned her doctorate in theology at the Pontificia

Universidad Javeriana in Bogotá, Colombia. She is a member of the research group in Moral Theology, eTHEOS, of the Universidad Iberoamericana and Catholic Theological Ethics in the World Church as well as founder and president of the Association of Graduates of Theology of the Universidad Iberoamericana (ASETI). As a specialist in human development, gestalt psychotherapy, and theology, she facilitates human development workshops, especially for women, vulnerable groups, and religious, as well as dedicating herself to psychotherapeutic practice.

Maria Teresa Gastón

Maria Teresa is an organizational psychologist and ICA certified ToP facilitator specializing in facilitation of collaborative discernment and decision-making. She received a BA in theology from Marquette University, an MA in Hispanic/Latinx theology and ministry through Barry University, and an MA/PhD in industrial/organizational psychology from the University of Nebraska Omaha. Maria Teresa served for many years in social ministry in Immokalee, Florida, and at Creighton University in Omaha, Nebraska. She and her spouse, John Witchger, have three sons and two grandchildren. Maria Teresa lives in Durham, North Carolina, where she directs Foundations of Christian Leadership, a formation program for Christian social innovators through Leadership Education at Duke Divinity School.

Katherine A. Greiner

Katherine A. Greiner is associate professor of theology at Carroll College in Helena, Montana. She holds a PhD in theology and education from Boston College. Her dissertation, "There Is a Wideness to God's University: Exploring and Embodying the Deep Stories, Wisdom, and Contributions of Women Religious in Catholic Higher Education," focuses on questions concerning Catholic identity, charism, and mission in Catholic colleges and universities founded and sponsored by women's religious congregations. Her research interests include Christian spirituality, lay ministry in the Catholic Church, and feminist and contextual theologies. She currently serves on the boards of the Conference for Mercy Higher Education and the College Theology Society. She has contributed to the *Daily Theology* blog and Liturgical Press's Loose Leaf Lectionary.

Antoinette Gutzler, MM

Antoinette Gutzler, a Maryknoll Sister from Queens, New York, holds a doctorate in systematic theology from Fordham University. She has served in mission both in Tanzania, East Africa, where she taught religion and worked with young students, and in Taiwan, where she directed a center for factory workers. After completing her studies in theology, she returned to Taiwan in 2001 and was associate professor of theology at Fu Jen University's St. Robert Bellarmine School of Theology in Taipei until her election to the Leadership Team of the Maryknoll Sisters in 2014. During her time in Taiwan she was a consultant to the Ecclesia of Women in Asia (EWA), a standing committee member of the Association of Major Religious Superiors, and a member of the Taiwan JPIC committee. Her recent publications include *Ecclesia of Women in Asia: Gathering the Voices of the Silenced* (edited with Evelyn Monteiro, SC).

Susan Haarman

Susan Haarman works at Loyola University Chicago's Center for Experiential Learning, facilitating faculty development and the service-learning program. She has degrees from Marquette University, Loyola University of Chicago, and the Jesuit School of Theology at Berkeley. In addition to having an MDiv, she also holds an MA in Community Counseling, a Certificate in directing the 19th Annotation of the Spiritual Exercises, and is currently a doctoral candidate in the philosophy of education. Her research focuses on the intersection between social justice education, civic identity, and imagination. She is also an improviser and licensed therapist in Chicago.

Nontando Hadebe

Dr. Nontando Hadebe is a lay woman theologian and senior lecturer at St. Augustine College in South Africa, specializing in African theology, pastoral and contextual theology, feminist and womanist theology, liberation theology, and pastoral psychology. She is a member of the Circle of Concerned African Women Theologians as well as the Theological Colloquium on Church, Religion and Society in Africa Women's Caucus, comprising Catholic women theologians in Africa. She was visiting fellow at the Jesuit School of Theology, Santa Clara University (August–December 2014) and Fulbright scholar in residence at Emmanuel College, Boston (January–May 2015). She co-edited a book published in August 2021 titled *A Time Like No Other: Covid-19 in Women's Voices,* which is a collection of women's stories and theologies during COVID-19 in South Africa.

Mary Catherine Hilkert, OP

Mary Catherine Hilkert, OP, a member of the Dominican Sisters of Peace, is professor of theology at the University of Notre Dame. A former president of the Catholic Theological Society of America (2005–2006), Sr. Hilkert is the recipient of four honorary degrees as well as the Washington Theological Union's Sophia Award for Theological Excellence in service of ministry in 1997; Barry University's Yves Congar Award for Theological Excellence in 2011; the Ann O'Hara Graff Award from the Catholic Theological Society of America in 2012 for her contributions to the integration of academic and pastoral theology with particular attention to the voices of women; and the Great Preacher Award from Aquinas Institute of Theology in 2021. She has written and edited several books and numerous articles for scholarly and pastoral journals. Currently she is working on a book titled *Words of Spirit and Life: Theology, Preaching and Spirituality.*

Rita L. Houlihan

Rita is a member of Ascension parish in New York City. She had a thirty-two year career at IBM in sales and change strategy consulting. She is on FutureChurch's board of directors and is committed to restoring our historical memory of early Christian women leaders with special advocacy for Mary Magdalene. In June 2015, working with a small group, she requested that Pope Francis issue a corrective teaching and elevate Mary Magdalene's memorial to a solemnity. A year later, the Vatican changed her memorial to a feast (a level below a solemnity) and issued a decree affirming her as the "Apostle of the Apostles" and an evangelizer. Rita initiated the "ReclaimMagdalene" project with FutureChurch in 2018. She has a BA in psychology and philosophy (Newton College of the Sacred Heart, now Boston College) and an MA in educational psychology from New York University.

Pauline Hovey
Born in Massachusetts, Pauline spent most of her life on the East Coast, until, in 2016, she felt a call in her heart too great to ignore, and she relocated to El Paso, Texas. Pauline first visited El Paso in 2013 on a border awareness trip sponsored by her church in Charlottesville, Virginia. The experience so moved her that she returned to El Paso to volunteer for several months at a time—first as a Tau volunteer with the School Sisters of St. Francis, and again in late 2014 through the end of April 2015 as a lay volunteer accompanying asylum seekers at houses of hospitality organized under the auspices of El Paso's Catholic-based Annunciation House. She continued to accompany asylum seekers until the first half of 2019. Her articles and essays have appeared on various Catholic online publications, including *National Catholic Reporter* and *US Catholic*.

Laurie Jurecki
Laurie Jurecki is a certified lay ecclesial minister in the Diocese of Cleveland and has been involved in professional pastoral ministry for thirty years. She holds an MA in theology from St. Mary Seminary in Cleveland. Raised Lutheran, Laurie Jurecki chose to join the Catholic community in 1978. She is a blessed

mom of four, grateful mother-in-law, and delighted grand-mother. In addition to having served as a pastoral minister, she has also served as a board member of Women and the Word—a preaching initiative that "creates a welcoming and supportive environment for the preaching of the Sunday Lectionary from a woman's perspective."

Marge Kloos, SC

Marge Kloos, SC, DMin is a Sister of Charity of Cincinnati and serves as a member of the Leadership Team of her religious community. As an associate professor at Mount St. Joseph University in Cincinnati, Marge has taught undergraduate and graduate courses in ministry, spirituality, pastoral care, and ecological and social justice. In 2008, she served as a scholar in residence at Tantur Ecumenical Institute for Theological Studies in Jerusalem, where she researched the impact of intergenerational trauma on women's spirituality. Having traveled with students to the US-Mexico Border, Cherokee Boundary in North Carolina, and Ireland, she has been enriched as a citizen and searching human through cross-cultural exchanges and learning. She currently serves on the boards of the Intercommunity Justice and Peace Center and Creative Aging Cincinnati. She holds degrees in environmental studies, theological studies, and ministry with a concentration in pastoral care.

Astrid Lobo Gajiwala

Astrid Lobo Gajiwala has a PhD in medicine and post-graduate diplomas in tissue banking, bioethics, and theology. She is a founding member of both Satyashodhak, a Mumbai-based feminist collaborative that contributes to the empowerment of women in the Indian Church, and the Indian Women's Theological Forum. She was a member of the Indian Theological Association (ITA) at a time when the majority of theologians were men, and served on their Executive Committee. She is a former assistant coordinator for Ecclesia of Women in Asia (EWA), which brings together women theologians from academia and the grass-roots; a former executive member of the ecumenical Indian Christian Women's Movement (ICWM); and former secretary of the Archdiocesan Pastoral Council. She is a resource person for the Federation of Asian Bishops' Conference and the Catholic Bishops' Conference of India, and a consultor for the Indian bishops' Commission for Women.

Léo Lushombo

Léo is an assistant professor of theological ethics at the Jesuit School of Theology of Santa Clara University. Originally from the Democratic Republic of Congo (DRC), she is fluent in French, Spanish, and English. She has worked as a consultant/formator with national and international NGOs in governance and gender programs, particularly on political participation in Peru, Cameroon, and the DRC. She has published several articles and book chapters, including a paper titled "Christological Foundations for Political Participation: Women in the Global South Building Agency as Risen Beings" (in the *Journal of Political Theology*) that strongly affirms the message: "Do not be afraid." She holds an MA in theological ethics from the Catholic Theological Union, Chicago, an MA in economics from the Jesuit Comillas Pontifical University (Spain), and a PhD in theological ethics from Boston College.

Crista Carrick Mahoney

Crista Mahoney, who earned her MDiv from Boston College School of Theology and Ministry (BC STM), began her professional ministry in campus ministry at Emmanuel College in Boston, Massachusetts, then as the Catholic chaplain on a multi-faith team at Babson College in Wellesley, before returning to her alma mater to work with students on retreats and women's faith sharing groups. In 2019, Crista finished her post-master's Certificate in Spiritual Formation at the BC STM. Her current primary ministry is accompanying individuals in spiritual direction from across the Christian tradition. Crista helped co-found the Jesuit Connection young adult group with the New England

Province of Jesuits and served on the board for Sacred Threads in Newton, a non-profit that offers women opportunities for spiritual nourishment, connection, and inspiration.

Jeannie Masterson, CSJ (deceased)

Jeannie Masterson, CSJ, spent many years of her life in Cincinnati, Ohio. Just prior to her death in 2019, she served on the leadership team of the Congregation of St. Joseph, a community created in 2007 by forming a union of seven founding groups of Sisters of St. Joseph located throughout the Midwest (including a Center in Japan). She earned a master's degree in spirituality from Fordham University, and she touched the lives of many through her generous service in education, vocation ministry, pastoral care, advocating for the working uninsured, and elected leadership.

Teresa Maya, CCVI

Sister Teresa Maya has been a member of the Congregation of the Sisters of Charity of the Incarnate Word, San Antonio, since 1994. Her ministry has been in education. She has served as teacher, history professor, and administrator. She has passion for the formation of ministers for Hispanics/Latinos in the United States. Sister Teresa earned her BA at Yale University, her MA at the Graduate Theological Union at Berkeley, and her PhD at El Colegio de Mexico in Mexico City. She is currently serving as congregational leader for her congregation and is a former president of the Leadership Conference of Women Religious (LCWR).

Rhonda Miska

Rhonda Miska is a lay ecclesial minister, writer, preacher, and spiritual director rooted in the Dominican tradition. She holds an MA in pastoral ministry from the Boston College School of Theology and Ministry (2011). She served as a Jesuit Volunteer in rural Nicaragua from 2002 to 2004, as the social justice minister/Hispanic minister at a Catholic parish from 2004 to 2008, and as the community coordinator of Innisfree Village (a lifesharing community with adults with intellectual disabilities) from 2008 to 2014. Rhonda is a contributor (as author and translator) to the book *Catholic Women Speak: Bringing Our Gifts to the Table* (Paulist Press, 2015) and also contributed to the book *Pope Francis Lexicon* (Liturgical Press, 2018). She currently serves on the advisory board of Catholic Women Preach and is the convener of the Catholic Women's Preaching Circle, a peer-led virtual space that provides Catholic women in ministry who are passionate about preaching the opportunity to develop their skills.

Catherine Mooney

Catherine Mooney teaches church history and the history of Christian spirituality at Boston College's School of Theology and Ministry. She has a master's in theological studies (MTS) from Harvard Divinity School, and an MA, MPhil, and PhD in medieval history from Yale University. She advances the study of saints in her roles as president of the Hagiography Society and as board member for the Jesuit-founded Bollandist Society. She serves also on the board for Monastic Matrix, a web resource centered on medieval women's religious communities, and has served on boards for the Society for Medieval Feminist Studies and the Franciscan Friars. Catherine Mooney's publications include *Gendered Voices: Medieval Saints and Their Interpreters* (1999), *Philippine Duchesne: A Woman with the Poor* (1990; 2007), and *Clare of Assisi and the Thirteenth-Century Church: Religious Women, Rules, and Resistance* (2016), which won the Hagiography Society's best book award in 2018.

Krisanne Vaillancourt Murphy

Krisanne is the executive director of Catholic Mobilizing Network (CMN), a national organization that mobilizes Catholics and all people of goodwill to value life over death, to end the use of the death penalty, to transform the U.S. criminal justice system from punitive to restorative, and to build capacity in U.S. society to engage in restorative practices. She previously served for more than a decade as a member of the senior church relations staff at Bread for the World, and from 2003 to 2005 she served as executive director of Witness for Peace. In the late 1990s, Krisanne was an associate with the Latin America Working Group, a religious coalition dedicated to mobilizing concerned citizens, organizations, and networks to call for a just foreign policy in the region. She has an MA in theology from the Weston Jesuit School of Theology. She and her husband reside in Washington, DC, with their three children.

Kate Ott

Dr. Kate Ott is a feminist Catholic scholar addressing the formation of moral communities with specializations in technology, youth and young adults, sexuality, pedagogy, and professional ethics. Her newest book is *Christian Ethics for a Digital Society.* Her other books include: *Sex + Faith: Talking with Your Child from Birth to Adolescence* and two co-edited volumes in addition to multiple book chapters and articles. She lectures and leads workshops across North America on technology and sexuality issues related to faith formation for teens, young adults, parents, and religious educators and professionals. She is associate professor of Christian social ethics at Drew University Theological School in Madison, New Jersey, and a lecturer in practical theology at Yale Divinity School in New Haven, Connecticut.

Sarah Attwood Otto

Sarah Otto earned her MDiv from Boston College School of Theology and Ministry. She graduated with a religious studies degree from Santa Clara University in 2007 and served a year with the Jesuit Volunteer Corps in Portland, Oregon. She is a retreat director and spiritual director at Ignatius House Jesuit Retreat Center in Atlanta, Georgia. Prior to retreat ministry, Sarah worked in college campus ministry at Providence College and directed the Newman Catholic Center in Chico, California. She and her husband (and fellow minister) Andy have two children who deepen their experience of the mystery of God in a myriad of ways!

Jamie T. Phelps, OP

An Adrian Dominican Sister since 1959, Sister Jamie is a theologian currently residing at the Dominican Life Center in Adrian, Michigan. She served as the Director of the Institute for Black Catholic Studies and was the Katharine Drexel Professor of Systematic Theology at Xavier University in New Orleans. Before that, she taught theology in Chicago at the Catholic Theological Union (CTU) from 1986 to 1998 and Loyola University from 1998 to 2003. Sister Jamie also served as a visiting professor of theology at the University of Dayton in Dayton, Ohio, from January to May, 2003, and twice at the University of Notre Dame: in 2005–2006 and 2012–2013.

Gerardette Philips, RSCJ

Sr. Gerardette Philips, RSCJ, was born in India. For the past twenty-one years she has been living and serving in Jakarta/Bandung, Indonesia, where she is the director of formation and district leader of the Religious of the Sacred Heart of Jesus. She is engaged in dialogue among people of different religions, particularly between Muslims and Catholics. Her master's and doctoral studies in Islamic philosophy and mysticism offered a new approach to dialogue. In 2005 she was appointed consultor to Pope Benedict XVI in the Pontifical Council of Interreligious Dialogue's Commission for Religious Relations with Muslims. In 2007 Sr. Gerardette was invited to be a speaker at the 62nd session of the General Assembly at the United Nations on Best Practices and Strategies for Interreligious and Intercultural Cooperation for Peace: Going Forward. Since 2009 she has been a lecturer at the Parahyangan Catholic University and since 2014 a lecturer on the Faculty of Religious Studies–Bandung State Islamic University.

Norma Pimentel, MJ

Norma Pimentel, a sister with the Missionaries of Jesus, is the executive director of Catholic Charities of the Rio Grande Valley. She leads the charitable arm of the Diocese of Brownsville, which engages in different ministries and services in the Rio Grande Valley through emergency assistance, homelessness prevention, disaster relief, clinical counseling, pregnancy care, food programs, and the Humanitarian Respite Center. Sister Pimentel's work is one of immediate response to the emerging needs in the community. Her humanitarian work on the U.S.-Mexico border, overseeing the provision of a safe space for migrants to rest and regain strength, has been recognized by many organizations across the country. She was named to the 2020 TIME 100 list of the most influential people in the world. Before overseeing Catholic Charities of the Rio Grande Valley, Sister Pimentel was one of the leaders who directed Casa Oscar Romero—a refugee shelter for Central Americans fleeing their war-torn countries. The shelter provided emergency relief and temporary housing for hundreds of thousands of refugees. Sister Norma Pimentel earned a bachelor's degree in fine arts from Pan American University, a master's degree in theology from St. Mary's University in San Antonio, Texas, and a master's degree in counseling psychology from Loyola University in Chicago, Ilinois.

Jacqueline Regan

Jackie is the author of "Every Picture Tells a Story: Imagining New Optics for Catholic Priesthood," in *Priestly Ministry and the People of God: Hopes and Horizons* (Orbis, 2022). She has served on executive boards for the Association of Theological Schools, the Association of Graduate Programs in Ministry, the Boston College Forum on Racial Justice, and the Regional Council of the Ignatian

Volunteer Corps. Jackie is the mother of two adult children, Maureen Emily (M.E.) and Tom. With gratitude for his active support of women in ministry, Jackie dedicates her contribution to this book to the memory of her husband Tom, who died of cancer in 2001. A former track and field athlete who has run internationally, she is a member of the hall of fame at the College of the Holy Cross and a proud Boston Marathon finisher.

Barbara E. Reid, OP

Barbara E. Reid, OP, is a Dominican Sister of Grand Rapids, Michigan. She holds a PhD in biblical studies from The Catholic University of America in Washington, DC, as well as an MA in religious studies and a BA from Aquinas College in Grand Rapids, Michigan. She is president of Catholic Theological Union in Chicago, where she is also Carroll Stuhlmueller, CP Distinguished Professor of New Testament Studies. Her most recent books are *Luke 1–9 and Luke 10–24* in the Wisdom Commentary series (Liturgical Press, 2021); *Wisdom's Feast: An Introduction to Feminist Interpretation of the Scriptures* (Eerdmans, 2016); and *Abiding Word: Sunday Reflections for Year A, B, C* (3 vols., Liturgical Press, 2011–2013). She is general editor for the fifty-eight-volume feminist commentary on the Bible, *Wisdom Commentary Series* (Liturgical Press). She is past president of the Catholic Biblical Association of America (2004–2005).

Yudith Pereira Rico, RJM

Sr. Yudith Pereira is a Spanish consecrated woman who belongs to the Congregation of the Religious of Jesus and Mary. Her academic background as agricultural engineer with a master's degree in education, expertise in spiritual accompaniment, and studies in theology and spirituality has facilitated a diverse ministry life carried out in Equatorial Guinea and Cameroon from 1995 to 2012. Her work has ranged from development projects related to education and women's empowerment to spiritual formation and accompaniment. From 2014 to 2018 she was the associate executive director of Solidarity with South Sudan, responsible for its international office in Rome. During 2021 she worked in educational development in Port au Prince, Haiti.

Kerry A. Robinson

Kerry Robinson is the founding executive director and global ambassador of Leadership Roundtable, dedicated to promoting excellence and best practices in the management, finances and human resource development of the Catholic Church by harnessing the managerial expertise and financial acumen of senior level lay executives. She has been an advisor to and trustee of numerous grantmaking foundations, family philanthropies, and charitable nonprofits, including the USCCB's Catholic Campaign for Human Development, America Media, the Jesuit Volunteer Corps, and the National Pastoral Life Center. She is the author of *Imagining Abundance: Fundraising, Philanthropy and a Spiritual Call to Service* and the founding editor of *The Catholic Funding Guide: A Directory of Resources for Catholic Activities.*

Virginia Saldanha

Virginia attributes her feminist roots to her experience of being a young widow in India. She taught catechetics in her parish school in Santa Cruz, Mumbai, for fourteen years, then completed a four-year certificate program in Theology for the Laity offered by the Bombay Archdiocesan seminary. She was part of the executive committee of the Archdiocesan Justice and Peace Commission; the first executive secretary of the Archdiocesan Women's Desk (1992–2000); the first executive secretary of the Women's Desk in the Federation of Asian Bishops' Conferences (FABC) (1996–2010); executive secretary of the Catholic Bishops' Conference of India Commission for Women (1998–2004); and executive secretary of the FABC Office of Laity and Family (2000–2010). She is the founding member and secretary of the Indian Women Theologians Forum and also the founding member and first executive secretary (2014–2018) of the Indian Christian Women's Movement. She is member of Ecclesia of Women in Asia.

Christine Schenk, CSJ

Sister Christine Schenk currently serves as a board member and contributing writer for the *National Catholic Reporter*. She is the author of two award-winning books. *Crispina and Her Sisters: Women and Authority in Early Christianity* (Fortress, 2017) details original research into iconic motifs of female authority found in ancient Christian funerary art. Her most recent book, *To Speak the Truth in Love: A Biography of Sr. Theresa Kane RSM* (Orbis Books 2019), documents an important period of Catholic history wherein women religious exercised unparalleled leadership on behalf of women's equality in the church. From 1990 to 2013, Sr. Chris served as cofounder and founding director of FutureChurch, an international coalition of parish-centered Catholics working for full participation of all Catholics in the life of the Church. A Sister of St. Joseph, she previously spent twenty years working as a nurse midwife in Cleveland.

Janet Schlichting, OP

Janet Schlichting, OP, of the Dominican Sisters of Peace is presently working in preaching, art, and adult faith formation. She has an MA in liturgical studies from the University of Notre Dame and a DMin in preaching from the Aquinas Institute of Theology. She has taught graduate courses in liturgy and preaching at Loyola/Chicago, Ursuline College, and Aquinas Institute and has served as a retreat center staff member and on Dominican preaching teams for parish missions and religious community retreats. She has written for pastoral liturgy and preaching publications.

Patricia Smith, RSM

A Sister of Mercy, Pat Smith received her BA in Latin education from Mount Saint Agnes College, Baltimore; her MA in theology from the University of San Francisco; and her PhD in theology from the University of St. Michael's College, Toronto. She was professor of theology and academic dean at St. Mary's Seminary and University, Baltimore, and served as community theologian for the Sisters of Mercy, Baltimore. From 2000 to 2008, Pat was vice-president of the Sisters of Mercy, Baltimore. For eight years, she was assistant to the president for Theology, Mission, and Ethics at Mercy Medical Center. Pat's academic interests include the formation of the scriptures, women in scripture, the Gospels, sacramental theology, and Mariology. She also speaks on Catherine McAuley, founder of the Sisters of Mercy. She is the author of *Teaching Sacraments* (Michael Glazier, 1985) and numerous articles.

Casey Stanton

Casey Stanton, MDiv, is the co-director of Discerning Deacons, a project committed to engaging Catholics in active discernment regarding women and the diaconate. She most recently served as adult faith formation minister at Immaculate Conception Parish in Durham, North Carolina. She holds a BA from the University of Notre Dame and her MDiv from Duke Divinity School where she graduated with a Certificate in Prison Studies. Casey spent a decade working in the field of faith-based labor organizing where she witnessed the power of collective action to bend decision makers toward justice. She hopes to be part of nudging the Church toward a more radical embodiment of inclusive leadership, hospitality, social action, and mutual care.

Cambria Tortorelli

Cambria Tortorelli is the president and CEO of the International Institute of Los Angeles, which helps newly arrived refugees and immigrants integrate into their new lives in southern California. Previously she served as the Parish Life Director (pastoral leader) at Holy Family Church in South Pasadena. Her previous leadership roles include assistant executive director of the Volunteer

Center of Los Angeles, president of Valley Interfaith Council, and moderator for the Archdiocesan Pastoral Council in Los Angeles. She is one of the founders of Fair Trade LA and in 2011 received the Ignatian Volunteer Corps Madonna della Strada award for her commitment to social justice. She has a BA in English language and literature from Oxford University in England and an MA in religious studies from Mount St. Mary's University in Los Angeles.

Sr. Nicole Trahan, FMI

Sr. Nicole Trahan, FMI, a native of Orange, Texas, is a member of the Daughters of Mary Immaculate (Marianists) and currently lives in Dayton, Ohio. Sr. Nicole serves her congregation as a member of the provincial leadership team, vocations director, and director of the pre-novitiate program. She is also a part-time campus minister at Chaminade Julienne Catholic High School. With master's degrees in Catholic school leadership and pastoral ministry, Sr. Nicole has a background in teaching theology/religion on the secondary level, collegiate and secondary campus ministry, retreat design and leadership, and spiritual accompaniment. She has a passion for faith formation and leadership development, especially of young people. This passion is equally matched by her dedication to seeking justice. She is also a regular contributor to *National Catholic Reporter's Global Sisters Report.*

Sister Jane Wakahiu, LSOSF

Sister Jane Wakahiu, LSOSF, PhD, is a member of the institute of the Little Sisters of Saint Francis, Kenya. Wakahiu provides leadership to and direction of the Conrad N. Hilton Foundation's Program Department and oversees planning, development, implementation, and evaluation of the Catholic Sisters Initiative. Prior to joining the foundation, Wakahiu was the executive director of the African Sisters Education Collaborative (ASEC). Wakahiu has taught extensively at the undergraduate and graduate level and has broad educational and administrative experience gained from serving as a teacher and administrator at a high school in Kenya and leading women's organizations. She authored *Transformative Partnerships: The Role of Agencies, Church and Religious Institutes in Promoting Strategic Social and Sustainable Change in Africa.* Wakahiu holds a PhD in human development and higher education administration from Marywood University, an MA from Saint Bonaventure University, and a bachelor of education from the Catholic University of Eastern Africa.

C. Vanessa White

Dr. C. Vanessa White, DMin, a Secular Franciscan, is associate professor of spirituality and ministry at Catholic Theological Union in Chicago and associate director of the Master of Theology program at Xavier University's Institute for Black Catholic Studies. She is a former convener/president for the Black Catholic Theological Symposium and her articles and essays have been widely published. She co-edited the book *Songs of Our Hearts and Meditations of Our Souls: Prayers for Black Catholics* (St. Anthony Messenger Press) and is a regular contributor to *Give Us This Day* (Liturgical Press). She is an advisor for the Fetzer Institute's Study of Spirituality in the Americas published in 2020 as well as a consultant to the USCCB's Subcommittee on Certification for Ecclesial Ministry and Service. She works with Bishop Joseph N. Perry in promotion of the cause of Venerable Fr. Augustus Tolton.